W9-BSC-799

A
House for
Jonnie O.

By Blossom Elfman

The Girls of Huntington House

A House for Jonnie O.

A
House for
Jonnie O.

Blossom Elfman

HOUGHTON MIFFLIN COMPANY

BOSTON
1977

3 -(1)-77

Library of Congress Cataloging in Publication Data
Elfman, Blossom.
    A house for Jonnie O.
    I. Title.
PZ4.E378Ho   [PS3555.L39]   813'.5'4   76-41689
ISBN 0-395-24901-5

Printed in the United States of America
C 10 9 8 7 6 5 4 3 2 1

To Milt

_____

The story of Jonnie O. is an answer to questions that plagued me during my two years with the Schoolage Expectant Mothers Program. Why were they having babies at *fourteen, fifteen, sixteen? Why were they keeping them?*

They were bused to the classroom on the *pregnant* bus to study English and history and math and government and child care and home arts. They were provided with a teacher and a nurse and a counselor.

They loved to crochet. As for the rest . . . they never listened. They were too busy listening to the requirements of their own hearts, or to the turning of their babies *in utero* . . . or to the endless discussions of what happened to *who* in the soap operas. I sometimes pounded the table to cut through their apathy. "Listen to me!"

Jonnie would casually open her *Silver Screen* and thumb through the pages for something of more value. "Why?" she asked. "What *for?*"

Contents

1

Promises, Promises

Yes. He had said *yes!* In the cramped phone booth with a door that wouldn't close, with the traffic roaring so that she had to jam the phone against her ear, she heard him say *yes!* She wanted to thank him, or tell him how she felt at least, but her three minutes were up. By the time she found the courage to say "I love you," the phone was dead. But her luck had changed! For once in her life, for *once* she had wanted something and asked for something, and *he had said yes!* Giddily, she hurried back to the classroom, wanting to feel the joy of it. She had been numb for so long. But how could she until she could touch wood to avert disaster. Wood—*where was wood?* A frail, dispirited bottlebrush tree stood in front of the dun-colored bungalow. A tree was wood, wasn't it? She ran to the tree and knocked on the thin, woody trunk. "Billy is coming back!" She said it to the tree. "He's coming."

She sank to the steps, limp with exhaustion. Now her head was beginning to ache, and her stomach felt funny. Wood was not enough. She needed something more, something,

1

*any*thing, one further confirmation to assure her that she and Fate were working hand in hand. She leaned back against the rough stone landing and opened her *Movie Life*. She turned to a page, *any* page, without looking, let her blind finger find the prophecy. It was a risk, because once you looked, there was no way out. You had to accept. But she needed to know — it had to be a sign. If it weren't, she might as well die!

Slowly she let her eyes drift down to the prophetic passage:

DON'T LET PREGNANCY MAKE YOU LESS
THAN YOUR BEAUTIFUL SELF!

Lainie Blake, starlet and mother-to-be, says: "The best time of my day is that hour when I luxuriate in my long soaky bath with the best of my bath oils. I don't just feel like a mother-to-be, I feel like a woman. And when Rod comes home from location, he wants to know he has a woman waiting for him." Lainie, fresh from her bath in a mauve peignoir . . .

It was a clear sign! She *thanked* the Fates that controlled her destiny. In gratitude, she promised to stop biting her nails. She promised to hold her temper for a week — she was too tired to think of anything else. She wondered, vaguely, if mauve were a color or a material. She thought of a hundred places she would rather be than where she was. She yearned to be in another time or space where she could feel like a woman after a long soaky bath. She turned her face to the small consolation of the morning sun and waited . . . until the sounds of traffic muffled and faded, until her fantasy transmuted them into the wild roar of waves, until she saw Billy's familiar figure coming toward her, running across the sand, calling her name, until she saw the clear Viking eyes, the crooked smile, the graceful carriage of his tall, thin frame, until he caught her in a passionate embrace and kissed her with lips still salt from the sea . . .

The door to the classroom scraped open on the landing. "Are you coming in or not?" asked the nurse.

Joanna Olson, recently sixteen, six months pregnant, shoved her *Movie Life* into her notebook. "Not," she said.

"And why not?" asked the nurse.

She flailed for a reason. They had to have a reason. "Because I *feel* rotten."

"Why do you feel rotten? Where do you feel rotten?"

Where — she tried to settle on a place that would satisfy them. "Heartburn," she said.

"And what did you eat for breakfast? Chocolate drink and a doughnut? So whose fault is it?"

She closed her eyes against the intrusion of this obsolete world.

"I don't want you sitting out here," said the nurse. "And it's too early to hassle. So either come inside or go home."

Inside meant a stupid movie and a stupid hour of Benjamin Franklin and a lesson in poetry, which she mortally hated. *Home* was worse. There was no way to beat it.

It rose in her suddenly, the quick flash of joy. *This isn't other mornings! Billy is coming!*

The Fates laughed silently. *Take care . . . he's coming . . . he's not here yet!*

She pulled herself up, rubbed the stiffness out of her back, picked up her things and went inside.

Hypocrites, with their big tolerance and understanding. They were so kind to you when you got pregnant. They listened and nodded and drowned you with sympathy. But you got big enough so that you had to wear a coat on a hot day,

3

and they got nervous just the same. If you didn't strip for gym for a month, they got edgy just the same. And they *suggested* you'd be happier in a *pregnant* school. For your own good. So you could be with other school-age expectants and have a nurse. It was a dreary stucco bungalow on a noisy traffic street. Not even a sign to mark it. Not even a flag. But it was a school, with the same tables and the same blackboards that made you sleepy when you looked at them. The same lessons that nobody gave a damn about. You could *die* between nine and three. The only thing that saved this little one room pregnant school was the tiny kitchen where you could make yourself a cup of coffee if you had to. And the bathroom where, if you convinced them that you were throwing up, you could hide and have a smoke at least. And you had friends.

Except for Ada and Maryanne, nobody looked up as she entered. Sometimes they hadn't slept well the night before so they slept now, heads down on tables. Or they painted their nails as they drifted and whispered. Or they diligently copied paragraphs, word for word, out of the *World Book* while they ate forbidden candy bars and drank Cokes from the security of brown paper bags.

Maryanne and Ada waved to her. Ada mouthed, "What happened?" Maryanne's eyes questioned dramatically. She said nothing, just walked casually to the table and dropped her books. It was still too risky, too fragile. It could still be snatched away. Such things happened.

Maryanne was going crazy. "Did you *call* him?" she whispered.

Jonnie nodded that she had.

"Is he *coming?*" Ada whispered.

She nodded that he was. Even that much of an admission

made her feel raw, as if her skin were peeled off, all her nerves exposed and electric. She felt edgy and shaky. "I need a smoke," she whispered.

"How?" whispered Ada.

"Where?" whispered Maryanne.

The nurse dimmed the lights for the morning film. The maddening drone of off-key school film music deadened the room. "Kitchen . . ." whispered Jonnie. "Let's go."

"Let's *not*," said the nurse, who was standing behind her chair. "Sit and listen for once."

She turned and looked at the hands of the clock, which were frozen in their sluggish circle. She slumped and half focused on the screen.

An old lady doctor leaned earnestly and confidentially toward them to explain about puberty. She would *die* if she had to sit through another lecture on puberty. The picture and the sound were not quite synchronized, so that the mouth spoke, but the words followed after, like an echo. And nobody had made the lady doctor *up* properly because her hair kept falling into her eyes.

"She should use Adorn," whispered Maryanne.

"If they got Bette Davis to play the part," whispered Ada, "somebody might listen."

Conception followed puberty. A cartoon *egg* dropped out of a cartoon *ovary* and floated down a *Fallopian tube*. The *penis erectus* was delicately drawn in little dotted lines, sending out its spray of *sperm*. The *sperm* was also delicately drawn, like Tinker Bell's magic dust.

She blanked out the film and tried to think about the way it really was. But it was too poignant, too bittersweet. Tears came to her eyes. So she settled for Barbra Streisand and Robert Redford. She was disturbed by rumors that Robert

5

Redford was short. People were always trying to bad-mouth the good stars. Barbra watched Robert so innocently asleep and he not knowing that she loved him. Barbra took off her clothes. Slowly, without waking him, she crept in beside him. He stirred to the movement of her warm body. On the screen a cartoon *egg* was empregnated by a single *sperm* and skittered over and attached itself to a *uterus*. Barbra moved her passionate body against his . . .

They all squinted up against the light.

"Questions," said the nurse, "let's have questions."

Alicia at the next table raised her hand. "Can I use the phone? *Please?*"

"No personal calls," said the nurse. "Call after school. Are there any questions?"

"But I need to use it now! It's im*por*tant!"

"So is conception. Please, this time ask questions."

"But this is a pregnant school! And I'm pregnant! So why can't I use the phone if I need to!"

"Since when," asked the nurse, "since *when* does pregnancy naturally require a phone? You must understand conception if we're going to talk about the Pill."

"She doesn't own the phone," grumbled Alicia. "So how come she *bosses* it! Anyway, you can't take the Pill. Pills give you cancer."

"You get holes from an IUD," said somebody.

"Better if you use Coca-Cola," said Alicia.

"How do you use Coca-Cola?" asked the startled nurse.

"Eggs is better," said somebody.

"Eggs? How on earth can you use *eggs?*"

"Whipped up," said somebody.

"Ladies," pleaded the nurse, "eggs whipped up or boiled or any other way are not contraceptive!"

"I'm *sick* again!" wailed Antoinette from the "slow" table. Antoinette usually got sick during the nurse's discussion. She was short and very round, with a moon face, wide-spaced teeth and lank hair. She made small animal noises when she got sick. She usually didn't make it to the bathroom and they died during English until the classroom aired out.

"Quick!" urged the nurse.

"Run!" yelled everybody.

Antoinette held a hand over her mouth and stumbled toward the bathroom.

"Saran Wrap," said Alicia.

"Please!" the nurse begged as she headed toward the bathroom. "Never let them use Saran Wrap! Saran Wrap comes un*wrapped!*"

They slipped into the little box of a kitchen. "Hypocrites!" Jonnie slammed the door and slid the bolt. "You could be dying for a smoke and they make you sneak around for it. But just look in their thermos! I'll bet you find Scotch!"

"Her?" Maryanne, who was very short with small hands and long fine pale yellow hair, squatted to get a pan out of the bottom cupboard. "She doesn't even *drink* coffee. I think she drinks *butter*milk or something."

Ada reached up to the cupboard for a can of soup. "Big fuss over nothing." She rummaged through the drawer of spoons for an opener. "Indians smoke peyote all the time to talk with the spirits." She emptied the soup into a pan. With a small gesture of her hand, she checked to see that the ends of her long braids were clear before she lit the fire. The ritual preparations were complete. They joined together. Jonnie unwrapped the brown cigarette from a handkerchief.

They were more than friends, the three of them. It was

Destiny that decreed that they should all three enter the classroom on the same day and Destiny that they should all three have got pregnant on approximately the same week, as far as they could figure. They sat together and ate together and went to shows together and talked together on the phone, and smoked together when the need was on them.

Jonnie held the cigarette for Ada to light. She shoved the counter of sack lunches aside and leaned back. She drew in smoke and waited for the sweet warmth to comfort her. Only when she released the smoke did she permit herself the luxury of speaking the words. "Billy Veller is coming back to L.A." The words gave substance to the reality. Now it was a fact.

Maryanne crossed herself before she took the cigarette. Maryanne was Catholic and very close to the Virgin Mary who watched over everything she did. "What did he say about you-know-what?" She drew in smoke. Her pale cheeks flushed red in two circles of color. It also happened when she was upset. It made her look like a painted doll. "What did he say — about the baby and all?"

"I had to promise I'd go to a doctor and ask could I still get rid of it."

"You're *crazy!*" screamed Maryanne.

"Keep it down," said Ada. "She was just asking. She didn't say she was doing."

"You're *crazy*." said Maryanne softer. "*I* wouldn't do it for *any* man, not even *think* about it. I'm not having an accident and dying and going to heaven and finding myself in trouble with God!"

"I *had* to!" said Jonnie. "It was long distance. What else could I say?"

"I couldn't even lie about it," said Maryanne. "When I lie, my hands break out."

8

"So I'll have to go and ask." Jonnie watched the burning end of the cigarette smoke and curl. "I'm scared."

"Who isn't," said Ada.

"I mean, how will he feel when he sees me this way? He said he was coming back anyway, but I'll never know now, not for sure." She played with that doubt, magnified it until tears blurred her eyes.

"He could have said *no*." said Ada sagely. Her wide cheeks and high forehead gave her a sort of stolid wisdom. Ada was the least volatile of the three. Things came to her slowly, but when she understood them finally, they settled in solid as rock. "Give him time. Some men, it takes them a little while to get used to it. Take my boyfriend. When he found out, he dragged me around to all his friends and bragged about it. Then when we were finally alone, he cried like a baby."

Maryanne fanned her face to cool it off. "Men . . ." She tugged her crucifix as she spoke. The Virgin turned to listen. "All the time we were in school, Arthur kept sending me these notes to come around and prove my love. So I went ahead and proved it because if you don't prove it, somebody else will, and I thought the Virgin would understand, being a woman and all. Then when he found *out*, when it was time for him to prove *his* love, he tells me he's underage and his mother won't sign for him."

"Billy's coming," said Jonnie, settling it in her mind. "That's all I care about."

They all knocked for luck.

Somebody knocked back. "Open *up* in there!"

They were going to drive her crazy if they didn't leave her alone! She shredded the remains of the cigarette and flushed it down the sink. "We're making *soup!*" she called out.

"Make soup with the door *open!*" warned the nurse.

"What do they want from me?" asked Jonnie. "They've got

9

me here, haven't they? I'm sitting and watching their dumb movies and listening to their stupid poems, so why aren't they satisfied to let me live, at least." Angrily she shuffled through the sack lunches until she found somebody's apple. She held the apple conspicuously behind her back.

"Open the door!" called the nurse.

Maryanne took down the cups and poured soup.

"You're terrible," laughed Ada.

Jonnie unlocked the door. The nurse peered suspiciously into the kitchen, sniffing the air to catch the scent, but the room was already redolent of the acrid odor of Campbell's Vegetable.

"Soup's ready." Ada casually took her cup and walked out.

Maryanne nervously fumbled and dropped a spoon. "Hail Mary." She crossed herself.

"Since *when* . . ." demanded the nurse, "since *when* do you say 'Hail Mary' for dropping a spoon?"

"Certain Catholics do." Maryanne scratched her hand, took her cup, and fled.

Jonnie leaned back against the counter, her hand behind her, and stared the nurse down.

"I have just cleaned up after Antoinette," said the nurse. "I feel like throw*upp*ing myself. I still have four home visits to make this morning. So don't play games with me, Jonnie."

"What games?" The nurse was gullible and pathetic. It was no contest. If they wanted somebody to handle the part, they should have got Jane Fonda.

"I wasn't born yesterday," said the nurse. "There are certain rules, discounting your health, which you choose to ignore."

"Since when do they have rules for making *soup?*"

"Don't provoke me. Just hand me what's behind your back and let's forget it."

10

Slowly, with great drama, she extended her arm and handed the nurse an apple.

She ambled back to her table to the roar of success. The nurse slammed into the office to make her usual complaints to the teacher. Antoinette, pale and exhausted, waddled over to Jonnie's table, carrying her fat notebook which everybody knew was filled with empty paper. Antoinette couldn't read or write. *"Please* can I sit here?" she wheezed in the way she did when she wanted something and was afraid she wouldn't get it. "I don't *feel* so good, Jonnie."

"She smells," said Maryanne. "Let her sit at her own table."

"It's okay." Jonnie made a place for her. "She's good luck."

Antoinette solemnly opened the notebook to an empty page, took a sharpened pencil, squinched up her moon face and leaned against Jonnie's arm. "Why can't I do things like the other children?" she asked plaintively.

"Hunger," said the teacher, "is the best pickle. Who said that. Alicia B.?"

Alicia, of the thick hair and the dark eyes and the large mobile mouth, looked up from where she had been resting her head on the table. "I can't *wait* until this afternoon to know. I need to use the phone! Jill is giving up her baby!"

There was a moan of distress from the class. *"Do you know for sure? When did she decide?"*

"She doesn't *want* to," said Alicia, "but she needs the money."

"Money?" The teacher was horrified. "She's taking money for relinquishing her baby?"

"She *has* to! Her father is dying of asthma and if she doesn't give her baby away to this older woman who's paying for her father to go to Arizona, her father will die!"

The class was angrily divided over the decision.

"But surely her father can go to Medical!"

"If you loved your father," said Alicia pointedly, "would *you* take a chance like that?"

"Call her!" urged the teacher. "Talk to her. Tell her she has alternatives. We'll send our own nurse over there. If she wants to give up her baby, let it be a free choice. There must be another way to save her father!"

The nurse was negating the suggestion from the office.

"Can't you go out there?" called the teacher urgently. "Can't you make a house call, under the circumstances?"

"The circumstances are from the script of 'Young and Restless,'" called the nurse.

The teacher was slow to take it in. She looked murder at Alicia. "This isn't your *sister* Jill? This isn't the Jill who is your stepsister? This is a chapter from a soap opera?"

"It comes on early. You can *die* until you find out at three o'clock."

The teacher slammed the table. "Who said that hunger is the best pickle?"

Nobody *knew* who said it. Nobody *cared* who said it.

"Why can't we have a television in the classroom?" asked Alicia. "Then one of us could watch and report."

"Hunger," said the teacher definitively, "is the best *pickle!*"

"Hunger isn't a pickle!" said Alicia. "If you're hungry, you *eat* a pickle. Why can't we go around the corner to McDonald's for a burger instead of bringing sack lunches?"

The class was ready to discuss it.

"First they tell us not to eat pickles," said Alicia. "And then they tell us *to* eat pickles. Why don't they make up their mind?"

"It's not nutritional advice. It's a literary comparison. Please

12

believe me, I don't give assignments in this class that aren't relevant. Didn't I spend an hour yesterday explaining how Benjamin Franklin got out of Boston by pretending he had got a girl pregnant, and didn't I explain to you that even Benjamin Franklin had children out of wedlock and one of them even wrote his biography? Didn't I give you all these interesting personal facts?"

"If he got a girl pregnant," said Alicia, "how come they made him President?"

"Benjamin Franklin was *never* President!"

"No wonder," said Alicia, "if he was all the time doing the nasties."

"What I'm trying to say," said the teacher, "what I'm trying to develop is that Benjamin Franklin, a historical hero, is simply a man like other men, like any of us. So why, when I gave you all these interesting human facts, did you all copy your paragraphs out of the *World Book?*"

"Shoo . . ." said somebody.

". . . and the exact same paragraph."

"That's *cold*," said somebody.

". . . and one paper wasn't even on the right Benjamin!"

"If we're finished," said Alicia, "can I at least call home and see if Jill looked at the baby before she decided?"

"Not this time!" said the teacher. "You're not getting away with it this time! Stick to the topic! Benjamin Franklin was a man who had a zest for life . . ."

"Zest is soap," said Antoinette proudly.

"Good try, Antoinette. What I'm trying to develop is that all of us have the potential to be Benjamin Franklins . . ."

The door shoved open. Thalia backed in carrying a car bed. "I'm here!" she announced.

Thalia, long-limbed and skinny, whose middle had been a

huge tight ball, was now almost flat. She hefted her car bed over to the history table, did a few dance steps to parade her new figure. "Fourteen hours' labor," she said majestically. "I felt when they cut me," she added proudly. "I bit the nurse when she sat me up for the spinal. You can get paralyze' from a spinal," she said ominously. She gave her hips a dance twist to demonstrate her joy and near escape. "Look and be jealous." She unfolded the blanket to reveal her sleeping baby. "Eight pounds four." She leaned over to kiss the baby. "You gettin' fat, you pig," Her voice scolded, but the pride was in her eyes.

The baby slept, curled in his tight sleep, little hammers of fists, tight oily ringlets of black hair.

"Thalia!" The nurse rushed out of the office. "What are you *doing* here? You just got home from the hospital!"

"Named him Delonne Rashay Two," said Thalia. "After his daddy."

"How did you *get* here?"

"Drove," said Thalia. "I'm okay."

Now the teacher was upset. "You don't have a license! You're not even scheduled to *go* until next week!"

"It's okay," Thalia assured her. "I got my learner's."

The nurse and the teacher hurried into the office to confer.

Thalia stepped back to allow the class to surround Delonne Rashay Two, to "oohh" and "aahh" and admire and to sigh with longing to see their own babies. Now she drew Jonnie aside. Now her smile faded. She looked tired and on the edge of tears. "Jonnie, I got trouble."

Jonnie's eyes were still on the baby. "He's so beautiful." But she saw the distress in Thalia's face. "He's not sick or anything?"

"My momma and my auntie are takin' him."

"How? How can they be taking him? He's your baby!"

14

"*I* know he's my baby," said Thalia. "*She* don't know he's my baby." Her eyes brimmed.

They all spotted her tears. Everybody wanted to know who had offended her. Everybody was on her side *without* knowing. Tears were a signal to tighten ranks. Thalia appealed to her supporters. "It's my baby! I suffered and I'm 'titled! And my momma is takin him!"

"She suffered!" roared voices. "She's 'titled!"

The teacher returned and tapped for attention. "Nobody at the history table except history people who are ready to work." It was a strong threat. They drained away. Except for the history people, who were watching the baby.

Thalia ran her long fingers over the fine crocheting of the baby's blanket. "Made by my own hands. You see them butterflies? I made them butterflies."

"Just let me finish launching Benjamin Franklin," said the teacher, "and then I'll open the crafts cupboard and you can *all* do butterflies."

Thalia dried the corners of her eyes with her fingertips. "I done Benjamin before I delivered."

"No you didn't," said the teacher. "Somebody loan Thalia some paper."

"Yes I *did!*" she flared. "I sent you my paragraph!"

"You did the wrong Benjamin."

"I did *not!*" she countered.

The teacher hesitated. "I'm sorry . . . but you did the Bible Benjamin instead of the history Benjamin."

Thalia considered the possibility. "Shoo, I thought it was funny he was born in the land of Canaan."

Delonne Rashay Two pulled up his legs, squeezed his face into a ball and made ready to squall. "He's gettin' hungry." marveled Thalia. "The doctor says he takin' too much milk. He got to take more water." She reached into the car bed for a

15

bottle of red liquid, uncapped it and let the girls watch how skillfully she touched it to the baby's cheek, how with blind eyes he moved his head cleverly to reach for the nipple and sucked.

"The whole idea of Benjamin Franklin," said the teacher, "was to bring you a man who had the courage to change his own destiny." Her eyes were on the bottle of red liquid. "His fortune was not in his stars but in himself." But the red bottle was bothering her. "Thalia, what are you giving the baby?"

"Water," said Thalia. "I *told* you. What you want I should write down?"

"Why is the water red?"

"He don' like it plain. I put Jell-o in it."

"*Jell-o?* You're giving a newborn baby *Jell-o?*"

Thalia half stood, angry and embarrassed. "You givin' somethin' or you ain't givin' somethin'!"

"But Jell-o has sugar and chemicals in it!"

Thalia appealed to the class. "He don' like it plain! I didn't know! And my stitches hurt!"

"Leave her alone!" said Jonnie. "It's *her baby!*"

The nurse was opening the door to two women, ushering them into the classroom. The larger of the two, still in her apron, stormed over to the table. "Fool!" she said to Thalia. She and the second woman hefted the car bed, tucked in the baby, grabbed Thalia by the arm. "Big fool!" They hauled Thalia off with them.

"Leave me be!" screamed Thalia. "He's my baby!"

When the door hissed shut, the classroom was silent. All silent.

"What did you *do?*" asked Jonnie incredulously. "Call her *mother?*"

"Let's break for nutrition," said the teacher.

The class was surly. They drifted away from the table to the

16

kitchen, opened lunches, whispering, discussing injustice and treachery, and the kind of behavior you might expect from teachers.

Only Jonnie remained at the history table, in place of Thalia, *for* Thalia. "Did you *have* to phone her? Did you get a *kick* out of doing that?"

"The baby was only five days old, Jonnie."

"But it's *her baby!*"

"Explain something to me," said the teacher. "Why is it I never hear a word out of you unless you're angry about something? Did you do the assignment I gave you yesterday? About Robert Frost? 'Two roads diverged in a yellow wood'?"

"I hate poetry. I never saw a yellow wood outside of a cartoon."

"I asked you what the two roads meant."

"One road is where *you* want to go," she said acidly. "And one road is where *they* want you to go. Anything *else* you want to know?"

"Yes. Why do you bother coming here day after day?"

It was no use. "Ask my social worker. She makes me."

"I really don't believe that," said the teacher. "What did Benjamin Franklin mean when he said that the squeaking wheel always got greased? What did he mean by that, Jonnie O.?"

"You want to know the truth?" said Jonnie. "I really don't give a damn."

"Scootch *down.*" The doctor's skinny pismire of a nurse settled Jonnie's heels firmly in the stirrups, looking at her with a sickly patronizing smile, as if she were some kind of juvenile freak. "You'd do doctor a favor if you wore socks," she whispered.

"Leave me alone, please!" Jonnie froze the bottom half of her body, turned herself into cardboard, trying to avoid the smiling, critical eyes. She didn't look up when the doctor came in.

"How's our patient today?"

"We're doing *fine*," said the nurse stickily.

"Will you get her to lay *off!*" begged Jonnie.

"I see you're in good shape today," said the doctor from *down there*, as usual making jokes while he intruded on the uttermost privacy of her body, prodding her as if she were a machine, some sort of robot, without feelings. The Bride of Frankenstein stood by and watched, clucking a tongue at her embarrassment. Chamber of horrors! She tried not to look at anything silver or metal or white. She conjured up a picture of her baby, floating like a fish in the warm ocean of her body. *You see*, she said to her baby, *you see what I'm letting them do to me? Only for you.*

"Good," said the doctor finally. "Sit up. Let's check that blood pressure."

She wrapped the sheet around herself, shoved away the fussing fidgeting nurse. "What month am I in?"

"Six," he said. "Maybe seven."

"Then it's really too late to get an abortion."

"*Abor*tion!" sputtered the nurse. "In our sixth *month!*"

She flamed with embarrassment. "Will you please tell her it's *my* sixth month and get her *out* of here before I throw *up* or something!"

The nurse was wounded; she fluttered, tightened up and walked offended out of the room.

The doctor wrapped the cuff of the pressure meter around her arm, not too gently. "Was that necessary?" He pumped the bulb, then released it. "If you're old enough to get pregnant, you're old enough to watch your tongue."

18

"For*get* it then." She tried not to meet his eyes.

He read the meter. "You know as well as she does that you're months too late. Having a baby at your age is a health risk, I told you that. But you stay up all night watching TV, you don't eat right, and now at this late date, you ask if you can get rid of it."

"I asked for an *abor*tion," she said helplessly, "not a *lec*ture? Don't have apoplexy about it."

He unwrapped the cuff. "You could have fooled me," he said. "I thought you wanted this baby."

"For*get* it!"

It wasn't worth the effort of an explanation. Let him do the mechanics. Let him check the pressure and measure the centimeters.

Somebody like Marcus Welby would have understood.

She didn't even expect her mother to be home. All she wanted was a shower and a change of clothes. Ada and Maryanne were waiting on the Mall. Just in and out, period. But the living room looked suspiciously in order. Fruit in the fruit bowl. Which meant that Abel was coming over. All she needed to make her day complete was Abel.

"Is that you?" her mother called.

"Who did you think it was?" She tried to escape to the bedroom.

Her mother stepped out into the hallway. "Abel is coming."

"Terrific," she said. "I'm going out."

Her mother followed her down the hallway. "Jonnie . . ."

"Don't worry about it. I'm going *out!*"

"I didn't *say* I wanted you to go out! All I'm asking is that for once don't be so rude. Just make a little pleasant conversation."

19

"I don't know how to make pleasant conversation. Just let me take a shower and I'll be out of your way."

"He's driving all the way down from San Diego to take me to dinner. Just say a word or two . . ."

"What am *I* supposed to do for dinner? Open a can of dog food or something?" She slammed the bedroom door and flopped down on her unmade bed. "Did I get any mail?" she called out.

Her mother opened the door. "I bought you a new maternity shirt."

"Doesn't it ever occur to you to knock?" She pulled off her shoes and dropped them to the floor. "I don't need a maternity shirt. Nobody under fifty is wearing maternity clothes."

"It won't hurt you to try it on. I put it in your dresser drawer."

"Did you come into my room again!" Jonnie exploded. "You *swore* to me!"

"All I did was put the new shirt in the drawer! What is there to snoop at? Just a bunch of old movie magazines. Please change into something nice and say hello to Abel."

"Okay! I'll say hello to Abel! Are you *sat*isfied? Now please just leave me alone!"

It was always the same. Her mother looked angry, then wounded, then her eyes settled on Jonnie's stomach, then remorse. She turned and walked out of the room finally.

Jonnie slammed the door again. What good did it do to close the door! No privacy! Nothing in that room that probably hadn't been pawed over, snooped at. The few objects that had any meaning to her life, all fingered and tossed aside as worthless, scorned as junk. She smoothed out her bed, sat on it, made a nest of blankets for herself. On the table beside her bed was the green glass egg. She warmed it in her hands, rubbed her fingers over the smooth surface and looked deeply into its center. The genie of Billy Veller was trapped in that egg. His image burned in her eyes. *An egg? This is all you want? Crazy kid . . .* She hadn't asked him for a gift. Nothing like that. She just wanted a thing to hold on to while he was gone. A small tangible thing. She had been so sunburned that day from lying on the sand, watching him sleep, etching the contours of his face into her memory, the way his hand lay open, the way his chest rose and fell. She could play it over and over again, evoked by the touchstone of the egg.

So she had an egg. What else did she have? A dime-store egg and a broken clock. When she was a child, when she believed in childish things, her father had given her a painted wooden clock. *Watch the clock.* Every time he left her. *Watch the clock. I'll be back.* But she wasn't a child anymore and she knew he wasn't coming back, and *why* he wasn't coming back. His letters didn't even come anymore. Her luck was bad. Even Billy hadn't come back, not until she phoned him. Maybe it was junk, all junk. Nothing of value in this house, no space belonging to her. Not this room, its limp curtains, its paper-shade dime-store lamp — all alien, all counterfeit. She lay on the bed staring up at the network of cracks on the ceiling until they began to take on ominous shapes. She held her baby, waited until it yawned and settled back to its nourishing sleep. Thoughts of her father intruded. It hurt her to remember. She didn't want to think about him. So she thought about Abel. She got up and opened the dresser drawer and took out the maternity shirt. Abel! Big joke Abel! No more like her father than a pale pitiful laughable imitation. Washed-out eyes. Schoolteacher smile. *Say hello to Abel!* She tossed her new smock on the bed and rummaged through her drawer until she found an old STP T-shirt. She pulled *that* taut over

21

her stomach, ran her hands through her hair to mess it up and walked out into the living room.

Abel, the nothing, nodded to her. "Hello, Jonnie."

Her mother almost died when she saw the T-shirt. "She just got home from school. She didn't have time to change."

"I changed." She fell into a chair, threw her leg over the arm and waggled her bare heel at Abel. "Hello, Abel!" she said enthusiastically. She turned to her mother. "I said hello to Abel. Can I leave now?"

"You *see* what she does!" her mother sputtered. "You see!"

"It's okay." Abel, smiling, leaned toward her, getting ready to make conversation. All she needed was conversation with Abel! "So, Jonnie. How goes it with you?"

Ada and Maryanne were waiting. But Abel gave her a pain. "Baby's growing. Makes me hungry all the time. Doctor says I don't eat enough. So where are we going for dinner? Okay if I come along like this? I haven't got anything else to wear."

"I just *bought* her a new shirt!" her mother protested. "You *see* how she acts!"

"I see you're both still at it," said Abel.

"Are you blaming me!" Now her mother's usual martyred face turned on Abel. "What do you expect from me! You'd have to have the patience of a saint . . ."

"She's a kid acting up. Have some sense of humor."

"Humor!" Her mother started to say something more, then walked in wounded justification out of the room. What Jonnie didn't need was Abel standing up for her. She gave him a saccharine smile. "Thanks for nothing."

"Look, Jonnie," said Abel, "give her a break. I know this has been rough on you, but she's had a hard time too. Give her a chance. Ease up on her."

"Who asked you to butt into personal business?"

"You've got her cornered," said Abel. "She's got nobody else to talk to. Just come halfway. Give an inch."

"Give an inch . . ." she mimicked. "Do me a favor. Leave me out of your wonderful conversations. Okay?"

"You see what she does!" called her mother from the kitchen.

"On second thought," said Jonnie, "you'd better eat without me. A little more of this and I'm going to puke."

She curled up on her bed until she heard them finish their *discussion* and leave. They were liars, all of them. Liars and hypocrites. She took off her T-shirt and put on the maternity shirt. To spite them. And she went to meet Maryanne and Ada on the Mall.

The one thing nobody could understand about Maryanne was Arthur Hammerman. He was under house arrest and his car was impounded, which meant that he had to take the public bus to and from school. All he could squeeze out for Maryanne were about ten minutes in Baskin-Robbins, which was near the bus stop on the Mall. It saddened her that a friend as close as Maryanne was stuck with Arthur Hammerman, who was an idiot.

Maryanne and Ada waved to her from their usual table. *"Please* be nice to him this time," begged Maryanne. "Don't bad-mouth him. He *means* well . . . it's his *mother* . . ."

It was hard to know what to say to Maryanne. "Can you just try to play it *cooler* or something?" She didn't want to be critical, but it was embarrassing.

Maryanne sat nervously watching the door, tugging on her crucifix, her face flushed into its painted-doll circles.

"So what are we going to see?" asked Ada. "Want to see *Godfather Two* again or *Towering Inferno* again?"

23

"I just don't want her to do what she did the last time," said Jonnie.

"I love *Towering Inferno* where he gets out of this helicopter and goes into this building, and his secretary says, 'I'm ready to take a letter now' and she opens a door to this room with a bed in it and satin sheets."

"It's *him*." whispered Maryanne.

Arthur Hammerman was tall, skinny, his long doleful face covered with acne. His chest caved in and his hands were bony and bluish as if he had just walked in out of the cold. He sauntered by as if he hadn't seen any of them, went to the counter and ordered a single strawberry cone.

"My cousin got satin sheets," said Ada, "for a wedding present. Trouble with satin sheets is they feel funny. And you can't wash them in the launderette. I'm not washing sheets by hand, not even for Paul Newman."

Arthur offhandedly fell into a vacant chair. Maryanne reached over to embrace him. "I tried to *phone* you."

Arthur looked nervously toward the window. "I asked you to stop *calling* me, Maryanne. My mother is having a *fit*."

"But I have to *talk* to you! It's getting *late!* Look how *big* I'm getting!"

"For Pete's *sake*," he begged. "Keep your voice down!"

"I waited since Monday! You *pro*mised . . ."

"I *know* I promised, but she's taking my car away for *good* if you don't stop calling."

"But I want to have the wedding before the baby comes." She started to cry.

"Have a heart." he pleaded. "Just stop calling until she cools down."

She dried her eyes with a paper napkin. "You promised to take me out."

"*Please* don't cry in Baskin-Robbins. I'll take you to a show or something next week. Only *please* stop calling me at the house!"

"Swear," she said. "Swear before God!"

"I swear, only stay away from the phone." He leaned over and kissed her cheek. "Okay?"

"I love you," she said passionately.

He handed her the melting cone. "She'll kill me if I'm fifteen minutes late. I have to go. So are you feeling okay, or what?"

"I'll feel okay as soon as we're married," she said tearfully.

"I have to go. Give me a break, Maryanne, and stop calling until I can get her to come around." He licked at the melting strawberry. "Want the cone or not?"

"Not," she said. "You know I hate strawberry. So will I see you tomorrow?"

"If I can. Take care."

"Some sport," said Ada, as they walked along the Mall eating triple chocolate.

"Please don't talk him down," begged Maryanne. "He means well. He wanted to talk to me. You *saw* that. It's her . . . I wish she would die." She crossed herself.

"You should never say love to somebody like Arthur," said Ada. "To Paul Newman maybe, but not to Arthur."

"Don't bad-mouth him." Maryanne bit tearfully into her cone. "You don't know him like I do."

They linked arms with her as they walked along, because in spite of Arthur, they understood her pain and anguish.

"He promised," said Maryanne, "and it's a sin to break a promise. But the trouble is he's Christian Science and they don't have a Hell. If they had a Hell, he'd marry me quick enough."

They stopped at Thrifty's to check their horoscopes in the

Times. Maryanne had to keep her business activities to a minimum in the P.M. Ada was expecting a visit from an old friend. Jonnie had to watch for subtle changes.

"What's sub-tile?"

Nobody knew.

But a cloud came in from the sea, ominous and damp, and hung over the corridor of the Mall. They decided on *Godfather II* out of loyalty to Al Pacino, because Paul Newman was older and had it made, but Al Pacino was short and still had a long way to go. They all knocked on the wooden ticket booth for luck. And they went in to see the show.

The glow of the film was still on her. She was reluctant to yield herself up to the oppressive semidarkness of the room. Her mother was sitting at the kitchen table, staring into a half-empty cup of coffee. She walked to the refrigerator, poured herself some milk, buttered herself a couple of slices of bread and spread them with jam. She could see her mother bitter around the lips as she looked at the maternity smock.

She pulled the crust off the bread before she bit into it. "Thanks for the shirt. It's neat." She drained the milk. "I'll wash my glass and put it away. Okay? I'm going to bed now."

"I want to talk to you." Ice in the voice.

"Not tonight, okay? The doctor says I need to sleep more."

"I don't want to argue and I don't want us both upset, Jonnie, but there are a few things we have to get straight."

"Tomorrow," said Jonnie.

"Tonight," said her mother.

She dropped into a chair, slumped at the table, closed her eyes against what she knew would inevitably follow.

"The least you can do is meet me halfway."

"*The least you can do . . .*" she echoed.

26

"Stop that!" said her mother. "Why can't we for once talk calmly and simply like other mothers and daughters?"

"Okay. What do you want to talk about? Abel? Did you ever take a good look at Abel? He's so dry and boring. I never heard him say three whole interesting words. But if that's what you want, it's your life."

"Why *is* it, Jonnie, why *is* it that any time a man tries to be decent to me, you act like a . . . a . . ."

". . . monster. You want Abel? So have him! Don't put it on me! I'm not stopping you!"

"Try to understand. You're almost a woman now."

She rolled her eyes dramatically toward the ceiling. "Al-*most!*"

"Your father is gone, Jonnie! He's not coming back!"

"Whose fault is that! You never stopped screaming at him!"

"What else could I *do* but scream. He never listened! Any more than you listen! He's gone. And I'm trying to make a life for us. You know I am! But every time things start to straighten out for us, you get yourself into some kind of trouble. Why, Jonnie!"

"I'm a troublemaker," she said. "So I'll get out and find my own place. I'll get out of here and you can have your puky Abel, if that's what you want!"

"Don't mix me up! Why do you always mix me up! Why don't you for once listen to me! You get pregnant and they give you a teacher and a social worker and a doctor making a cruddy fuss over you! But nobody gives you a good smack on the behind for being a brat!"

". . . which of course I am!"

". . . which you are!"

"So why don't you get pregnant?" said Jonnie. "Then they can make a fuss over you!"

27

"There's no use trying to talk sense to you. You have to accept that your father isn't coming back. We hardly ever hear from your father anymore."

"Hardly . . ." She felt her face flush. "You said never! Hardly means sometimes! When did you hear from my father? I'll bet he wrote! I'll bet you know where he is!"

"I haven't heard . . ."

"You said hardly! I'll bet he wrote and you tore it up because you're so jealous that he writes to me and not you!"

"What makes you lie like that?" asked her mother bitterly.

"Now I'm a liar! I'm a monster and a liar and a brat! What else am I? I just love these nice little mother-daughter talks we have."

"Well whose fault is it! You push me to the limits!"

"Right. You're Mrs. Tolerance. They'll make you mother-of-the-year because of all your sacrifices. Come on, what else am I?"

Her mother looked into the cold dregs of the coffee. "You're a thief."

"Thief! Where am I a *thief!*"

Her mother lit a cigarette. "There's no use trying to talk sense to you. You're just like him. He was a rock. You could die in front of him and he'd walk right over you. You listen to me this time, Jonnie. This time I have something good going for me, and I'm not giving it up. I won't let you spoil it this time."

"*Where?*" she screamed. "Where am I a *thief?*"

"I don't want to talk about it. Go to bed."

"You wanted to talk about it before! You were dying to talk about it before! Now you just talk about it and tell me where I'm a *thief!*"

"I have nothing left from that marriage, Jonnie! Not even memories. I saved a few things, things of no value to anybody but me. Things that were mine . . ."

Her face went hot. "You came into my room again! You *pro*mised!"

"I only went into your room because it was a rat's nest. I thought I'd do you a favor by cleaning it out. I found them in the closet."

Now she saw them on the sink, the blue china cups with the flowered rims. She felt a pain swell in her chest.

"The cups were all I had left. Can you understand that, Jonnie? A box of blue cups, after sixteen years. But they were mine. They meant something to me. If you had asked at least . . ."

Suddenly she couldn't breathe. "They were *his* cups *too*! They're mine as well as yours!" She shoved away from the table, heat in her face as she looked at the cups. "I'm getting out of here! I don't need you to sacrifice your crummy fingers to the bone . . ."

"Don't you?" cried her mother. "Don't you? You're only sixteen, so everybody *expects* you to spend half your life lying in the bathtub reading movie magazines and daydreaming, but *somebody* will have to take care of that baby, and *somebody* will have to feed that baby and *somebody* will have to diaper that baby . . ."

"Shut *up!*" she screamed.

"All right. *Think* of yourself. Take the cups if you want them that much, but once, just once, give me a chance."

"*Who* thinks of herself!" she screamed. "Who? You messed things up for yourself, and *you* messed things up for my father, and now you're messing things up for me! Well, I'm getting out of here and I don't need you and I don't need your crummy sacrifices, and I don't need your crummy cups!" She ran to the sink and took a blue cup in her hand.

"Oh please!" begged her mother. "*Please* don't . . ."

A House for Jonnie O.

She struck the cup against the sink. The sound, in the momentary inbreath of silence, was almost musical. The pieces fell to the floor. She held the handle out to her mother. "Who needs your cups. Anyhow, this one's cracked."

She left her mother picking up the pieces. She ran out of the room, holding in the explosion. She tried to lock her bedroom door. *Nothing* locked! No place where she could escape! She pushed a chair against the door and turned on the light. The pain in her chest welled. She tightened against it. Her room was a cave, a cavern — the cracked ceiling, the tacky shade — the room and everything *in* it made her sick. She felt hot and swollen. Tears burned against her eyes but she forced them back. She lay on her bed trying to block it all out. She leaned over and spoke to her stomach. "Don't worry . . . we'll be all right . . . " Her throat was a tourniquet. Her tongue burned. Tears scalded her eyes, but she would die before she let anybody hear her cry. She wished she could explode into a million stars and be anonymous in the dark night. Her baby turned inside her. The room was a prison. The closet door, which never quite closed, rumbled with the monsters who waited in those deep hidden places and rattled and threatened in the night when she couldn't sleep. On the walls around her, her old friends, her constant friends, stared softly down. Mia Farrow, and Shirley Jones, and Diahann Carroll, and Elizabeth Taylor, and Bette Davis, and Olivia de Havilland, all the women who got what they wanted, who had space around them and clothes that glittered, and men who came to them with open arms, and smiles on their faces, and breakfasts in bed with somebody who brought you a tray with a fragile china cup. *It wasn't fair!* She wanted her father. She needed her father. She needed to be held and comforted, for somebody to put a cheek against her face and kiss her and ease the hurt. For a moment, for one bright palpable flash of a moment, she *had* him! *Poor Jonnie,* whispered his voice, like a rush of wind, and then, with a sigh, she lost him. *Gone!* Leaving her a terrible void, an emptiness that pressed in on her like death, a chasm of nothing, cold space, alone. *It wasn't fair!* The cry burst out of her. Tears crested and broke. She sobbed, out of control, possessed entirely by anguish, adrift in it. She held a pillow over her face to muffle the sound. *Help me!* She flailed for something, *any*thing, any spar to keep her from drowning.

She remembered. *Billy was coming!*

The Fates murmured and laughed. *But you had to call him, didn't you.* It wasn't *fair!*

She wept until the tears played themself out, until her breath caught in little afterthoughts of pain. She pulled herself up, exhausted, and turned off the sharp accusing glare of light. She lay back, holding her baby.

Her baby!

But she had her baby, didn't she? Nobody could take her baby away from her.

The room was softened by the light of the moon through the curtains of her window. Inside her, the baby turned and slept again. From the wall above her, the eyes of Olivia de Havilland looked down with tenderness and compassion. She curled in the soft darkness with her baby and waited for some fantasy to obliterate the truth.

2

Home Is the Hunter

SHE WAS all at once awake! *Please* let her face not have broken out during the night. She touched the wood of her headboard before she got the nerve to get up and look into the mirror. Gave thanks for that, at least. But she searched her face to see how much she might have changed. She was too pale, all her summer color faded. And she had done such a dumb thing by cutting her hair so short, *stupid* to have cut her hair like that. Black thick uncurling hair. Long, it lay across her shoulders at least. Now, this way, if she slept crooked, it went back on her and stuck out. Ridiculous. She had to pull at it to get it down over her ears. And her *nails* were bitten. She was sure she'd have time to grow them out. Now she was stuck with stubby fingers. She checked the clock to see if there was time to make improvements. She tried to smile into the mirror. If she held her mouth in a certain way, she could sometimes get that arty Liza Minnelli look, but now her face wouldn't even *smile*. She walked silently down the hall, trying not to wake her mother. She latched the bathroom door and stood on the toilet seat to check her body profile. The baby had been giving her a little shape at the top. Now her stomach was getting so huge that the benefit was overshadowed. She climbed down and practiced walking with her shoulders back to try to look normal. Useless. Her short hair, her ears sticking out, her pale face that made her eyes look about three sizes too big. She didn't look like a woman, she looked like a pregnant boy! Nothing would make her look the way she looked when he had seen her last.

She took a quiet shower and walked silently into the kitchen, hoping to eat and escape. But her mother was already sitting at the kitchen table, drinking coffee and smoking a pack of cigarettes.

She poured herself a glass of chocolate drink, too nervous to eat.

"Is that all you're taking for breakfast?"

She didn't want to hassle. Not *this* morning. She dropped a piece of bread into the toaster, waited nervously for it to brown. It caught in the wires and started to burn. She flicked it up, tried to wedge it out with a knife.

"Don't *do* that! You'll *kill* yourself if you put a knife in that thing."

"That ought to solve your problems." She scraped the burned toast, buttered it, gulped it down with the rest of the chocolate. She rinsed the glass. "I washed my glass." She held it up for inspection before an unseen audience. "I want you to see that I washed it. So that you don't have to stay home for hours cleaning up after me."

Her mother rubbed the cigarette out in a saucer. "Don't do that anymore, Jonnie. Please, I mean it. I can't take it anymore. Meet me halfway. I'm willing to go *more* than halfway. You want me to say I'm sorry? I *am* sorry. I mean it. I'm sorry for last night. For once, *talk* to me."

"Talk to Abel. He's full of marvelous conversation."

"I want to talk to *you!* You make me feel like a pressure cooker! For once listen to me! For once, smile and say something nice to me."

"Sure." She smiled the bland innocuous smile of grocery clerks. "Have a nice day."

In the little park, which was actually a patch of grass with two benches, a tree, and a trash can, she explained it all to her baby. It was easy to talk to her baby. The thoughts drifted from her head to her baby without the impediment of words — in a rush of feelings. She could summon people when she needed them — to take her side, or to plead her case. Her father came forward as a sympathetic witness. He spoke for her, explained for her. People came to stand accused, justice was dispensed, she was vindicated. Her baby listened, understood, responded with a movement of an arm or a leg, and then turned to sleep safe in the pouch of her body.

She saved Billy for last, savored him for the best. She replayed it the way she had replayed it a hundred times. She sat in a room, a beautiful room, waiting for him to come. Her hair was long now, lying across the shoulders of her mauve peignoir. Her body was a slim woman's body. In its little painted bed, her baby lay asleep. Someone knocked. She knew that knock. He stood there in the doorway, trembling with desire for her. He took her in his rough arms, held her passionately. *Jonnie,* he moaned. *Billy,* she murmured. From the little painted bed, a child's cry. He looked up, startled. *Yes,* she nodded. Gently, she led him to where their baby lay.

"God," said the voice, "look at you!"

She jumped, tried to focus out of her fantasy.

"Jonnie?"

34

It wasn't *fair!* She wasn't *ready!* She didn't have time to prepare herself. And the voice that had spoken, *his* voice, came from a stranger! From a tall thin stranger in dirty denims, a tall unshaven figure with mud-caked shoes and grimy hands. Cold panic spread to her stomach. Her hands turned ice.

"I can't *believe* it! What *happened!*" he asked.

Her disappointment turned to anger. "You can see what happened!"

"Why?" he asked incredulously. "Why didn't you just get rid of it when you found out? It's nothing to get rid of it. How could you be dumb enough to wait this long?"

"Why did you wait this long without *calling* me!" she accused.

He started to explain something, but didn't. "I couldn't call."

"Why couldn't you? Was your arm broken or something?" It was spoiled now — all of it. She was the fool — she —

"Honey, I couldn't call! I was stuck in a shack in the mountains twenty miles from a phone!"

"What shack! You were on a fancy ranch training horses for the movies! You and your friends!"

"Friends," he snorted. "Some friends. It didn't work out for me. I was stuck up there without a buck. I was sweating it out on a sheep ranch until I had enough money to stake me for something else."

"It's not *true!*" she accused. "You were there when I phoned you!"

"I just stopped by to pick up some gear. It was a hundred-to-one shot that you caught me."

The Fates murmured.

"Five minutes later and I would have been gone, honey."

35

He seemed so weary. He sat on the bench beside her, his head resting on his arm as he looked at her. "I couldn't call," he said again. "But I thought about you, Jonnie. You were the only decent thing that happened to me all year." His voice softened and he spoke with sympathy. "Why didn't you just get rid of it, honey? It would have been so easy."

The sound of his voice, the edge of it — he was beginning to sound familiar. She looked hard to see Billy Veller in this stranger, this tall thin boy with the tired face and the blackened dirt-gritted hands. "I wanted to," she said. "I waited for you to call, to talk it over . . . I waited for months."

"I had bad luck, Jonnie. Rotten luck. Can you understand that?"

"Then why didn't you phone me? When you had the bad luck, why didn't you call me? I waited so long for you to call. I almost died every day when you didn't. I figured that when you called, we'd talk it over. I was afraid to go by myself. Then, when I found out for sure and you didn't call me anymore, when I knew you'd dumped me . . . "

He touched her shoulder with his hand. A gentle hand, the way she remembered. "Come on," he said. "Come on . . . don't say that."

Her accusation had hurt him. When she saw the hurt in his eyes, the warm place reserved for him in her heart stirred to life again. "You didn't call me and I was alone, and I thought you weren't coming back. And one day the baby moved, and I knew it was you. You were gone. And the baby was all I had left, Billy."

His eyes on her were so soft now, she couldn't stand it. He studied her face as if he were also looking for the stranger in her. "You cut your hair. Why did you have to cut your hair?" She could have died. Now she could see Billy. Now she could

36

see the familiar sadness in his eyes, the crazy smile. *You don't know*, murmured the Fates. *You never know . . .*

"Did you ask the doctor? You said you'd ask the doctor."

"I asked him yesterday. It's too late . . . " She buried her face in the rough denim of his jacket. She touched the solidity of Billy Veller. "I almost died without you, Billy. I couldn't stand it."

"You're such a funny kid," he said. "You couldn't get rid of it because you loved me, you really loved me."

She wanted to say it to him. But she was afraid. She wanted to say she loved him. She wanted to tell him that the world without him was a gray world, an empty world, that he was worth the pain, and the bittersweet longing, and the waiting, and the praying, and the danger, and the caprice of chance, begging for luck to throw just one scrap in your direction. Nobody understood that. Maryanne and Ada were still children. Elizabeth Taylor, *she* understood it, the sad lines of her aging face, suffering without Richard. Mia Farrow understood, that sad little enigmatic smile. This was the love women felt, *real* women.

"If you love me, I guess you're the only one who does, Jonnie."

She couldn't bear to see his eyes when he said it. "I've had bad luck too, Billy! But my luck is changing. The baby is changing my luck."

"Honey," he pleaded. "Give me a break. What am I going to do with a baby? I haven't got a buck in my pocket."

She answered with caution. "It's okay. I can always give it away after. But stay with me until it comes, Billy. I'm scared."

He said he knew what it meant to be scared. He held her to make her feel better. And then he held her for his own sake. A woman knew when that happened. She felt it, the way she felt it last summer when she knew he needed her. "Two peas in a pod," he said. "We both have such rotten luck. Luck waves her hand at you, you go running to catch her, and she turns around and kicks you in the teeth. Why is it?"

She tried to put his hand on the baby. "Touch it, for luck."

He drew his hand away. "Not if we're giving it up."

He had said we. *Billy was back!* She jumped on him and hugged him and kissed him. She was worse than Maryanne. They fell to the grass and rolled around like puppies, happy to be together again. *It was right, what she had done. She knew that now.*

He sat up finally, and they looked at each other. He was handsome, eyes clear as glass, green like the egg, with that certain sadness that used to remind her of James Dean, but even now she put the thought aside. She didn't want to mix her burgeoning good luck with dead stars. She wanted to hold him, to have him forever the way she had her baby.

"I hate this town," he said. "They make you promises in this town, and they always let you down."

"Not me, Billy. I'll never let you down."

"I'll look for a place to crash," he told her. "I'll call you."

She returned to the world of children.

She waited impatiently on the corner for the pregnant bus. It ground to a stop. She swung aboard and waved jubilantly to Ada and Maryanne. "Good news." she called out.

"Bad news," said Ada.

She lowered herself into a seat. Maryanne and Ada turned around to face her, knees on the seat, bellies against the back.

"Her boyfriend got picked up," said Maryanne.

"Picked up for *what?*" She prayed it wasn't her fault, her

good luck pulling against Ada's. She looked for wood to touch, but everything on that bus was metal or plastic. "For *what* did they pick him up?"

"For nothing," said Ada morosely. "For a busted head-light."

"I told you ladies to sit front!" called Mrs. Osley, who drove the pregnant bus. "I told them downtown that I wasn't going to drive unless you sat proper! If you think you're going to fall down and collect the insurance, you've got another think coming!"

"How can they pick him up for a broken *head*light?"

"They asked him for his registration," said Ada. "All he did was reach over to the glove compartment and something fell out of his pocket."

"What?" asked Jonnie. "What fell?"

"Don't ask," said Maryanne.

"It wasn't even for him," said Ada. "He was taking it to a sick friend. The only reason they picked him up is because he's an Indian. Just look at all the crazy stuff people do and get away with it. If you're somebody, or the son of some-body, they let you get away with murder. Look at Kung Fu. He goes crazy on dope and crashes through windows and stuff and nobody picks up on him because he's Chinese. If he was an Indian, they'd kill him. My boyfriend tried to tell them he was grandson of a chief and a full-blood Oglala. They thought he was trying to make another Custer's Last Stand. They handcuffed him and pulled him in."

"He's finished," said Alicia, from across the aisle. "Better get yourself a new boyfriend."

"I'll never find another man like him. You know how long I've been hearing stories of Indians from my grandmother? All my life she's been telling me stories about the land of my

39

people. I wanted an Indian to be father to my baby. I wanted
it to be like my grandmother said. *Only* marry a full-blood Indian, she said. I loved that old lady. She was the only one
ever gave a damn about me. So I prayed for a full-blood Indian. I didn't want any piece of an Indian or part of an Indian.
I wanted full-blood. My luck, the only full-blood Indian I find
in L.A. is on the streets. I got him off the streets. He's got a
bad thread in him."

"Does he have a lawyer?" asked Jonnie.

"It's going to take more than a lawyer," said Ada bleakly.
"I've got to get him back to the land of my people."

"Where's the land of your people?" asked Alicia from
across the aisle.

"Dakota," said Ada.

"How's she gonna get to Dakota?" asked Alicia. "I'm Mexi-
can. I ain't even been to Tijuana."

"A lawyer will cost," said Jonnie. "Got anything left out of
this month's check?"

Ada turned around, slumped in her seat. "Who's got
money left? He took it and spent it on a sick friend." The
pregnant bus rumbled through the city streets. "He's got a
bad thread in him. I've got to pull it out."

The nurse was upset because they were going on a field trip
and nobody had remembered to bring in their trip slips. The
teacher was writing the Bill of Rights on the board. Just what
nobody needed was the Bill of *Rights* again. There were more
important topics to discuss.

Alicia, their chief source of current events, was explaining
in detail what happened to her friend who woke up in the
middle of the night and found these two bare feet standing
next to her bed. Somebody had found a new remedy for flatu-

40

lence, especially after eating pizza. Somebody heard about somebody who had a *tubular pregnancy*. They all tried to figure out what was a *tubular pregnancy*.

The nurse tapped for attention. "Let's face it. We cannot go on a field trip without a signed trip slip, so if you're intending to go, get your trip slip signed by your mother or your father or your guardian and bring your own sack lunch. They provide the punch."

"Do they show the good movie?" asked Alicia.

"They show you *a* movie," said the nurse. "They do not show you *that* movie."

"That's a boss movie," said Alicia. "My sister saw it."

"Three girls fainted from that boss movie."

"We seen worse in *Jaws*," said somebody.

"A movie about delivery with a frank episiotomy does not have to be as bloody as a movie about sharks," said the nurse. Even *I* can't stand to watch that movie. It's just not necessary. When the time comes, you won't feel it."

"Yes you *do*," said Alicia. "My mother had a Caesarean and they cut her open and her insides popped out and she felt the whole thing."

"That is absolutely not *true!*" said the nurse.

"It is *so* true! Were you there? She felt it and I was the baby and now I have to appreciate how she suffered for me."

"Please stop telling horror stories, and get the trip slips signed."

"What if you're not living with your mother?" asked somebody.

"Then have your father sign it."

"What if you're not living with your father?"

"Then have your husband sign it."

"What if you're living, but he's not your husband?"

"Then forge it. Why *is* it" asked the nurse, "that I have the answers to a thousand important questions, and *these* are the questions you ask me? We're going on a field trip to the hospital. You'll see the admission process, you'll visit the nursery, including the preemies, and the labor and delivery rooms . . ."

"With somebody having a baby?" asked somebody.

"Would you like to deliver a baby with a class of pregnant girls watching?"

The door scraped open. Thalia slammed it shut, leaned against it, stared with slitted eyes first at the nurse and then at the teacher. Thalia, in a pair of leather tight-crotched shorts and a fishnet blouse without a bra, swinging a purse, and angry. Everybody sat up, *awake!* It was going to be a worthwhile morning.

The teacher had just finished her Bill of Rights. Now she put down her chalk and looked a question at the nurse.

Thalia walked slowly, dramatically, across the room, swinging her hips and purse. She tossed the purse down on the history table and dropped into a chair, focusing her slow, simmering anger on the teacher.

Jonnie and Ada crowded next to her to give support. The whole class was in essence *with* her, for what*ever* reason. It was seldom that anybody had the luxury of anger, and to hook into a real one was worth the effort.

"I'm glad you're back," said the teacher. "I tried to phone you."

Thalia's eyes remained pinned on the teacher's face. She was silent.

"Why don't we get on with the right to pursue happiness," said the teacher, "and then you and I can talk during nutrition."

42

Thalia stared in classic form. Her eyes remained constant. Only her foot tapped out the slow rhythm of her anger.

"The right to pursue happiness " — the teacher spoke to the class at large — "was promised to us in the Declaration of Independence."

"Try to pursue happiness," said Jonnie. "Just try it!"

The teacher shot her a warning glance, then turned her attention back to Thalia. "Would you like to borrow some paper so that you can take notes with us?"

Thalia said nothing.

"The teacher is *talking* to you," said Jonnie sarcastically, staring with Thalia at the teacher.

"No she ain't," said Thalia, keeping her eyes fixed. "She ain't talkin' to *me*."

"I'd like to discuss the human right to pursue happiness and your legal rights as pregnant women," said the teacher.

"Ain't got no rights," said Thalia, *"have* I?"

"When you got pregnant," said the teacher, "in the eyes of the law you became emancipated minors, which means that you can sign for your own medical care, and even for your own abortion."

"That's what you all want, ain't it," said Thalia. "Kill off the black babies."

The teacher's face flamed. "That's not what I meant and you know it."

Thalia had scored a palpable hit. She pressed her advantage. "Just like the old days — sell us like cows! Martin Luther *King!"* she accused.

"Why don't you ever *listen* to me!" The teacher was cracking first. "I'm trying to tell you that I under*stand* your need to pursue happiness, but I'm bound by certain obligations, Thalia, just as you are."

43

Thalia floundered for a comeback, found none. "Why don't you just shut up!" She said finally.

That was too strong. That was a confrontation. There was total silence while they waited for the response.

"If you don't want to listen," said the teacher, "why bother coming . . . "

"Not to talk to you!" said Thalia. "I'm suppose to go for my license. So why don't you shut up and leave me alone!"

"Ooohhh," said the class. "That's cold!"

According to the rules of the game, things were never allowed to get that bad. The teacher was in an awkward place. And she was losing patience. She looked at Thalia's blouse. "Like *that* you're going to the Motor Vehicles?"

"Like *what?*" Thalia demanded.

The teacher was already beyond the point where she could give a tactful answer. "You can't go to the Motor Vehicles with *naked breasts!*"

The class waited anxiously, enthusiastically to hear Thalia's return shot. *Naked breasts* was a powerful blow. Thalia had a cold cut coming. Anything went at this point. They all sat forward, adrenalin flowing, formulating their own put-downs. Like *Why not? I don't drive with my tits!* But Thalia was flustered. Her eyes crept down to her blouse. "What's *wrong* with it?" she sputtered. She broke into tears of embarrassment and fled to the bathroom. The game was lost.

The history table followed her, except for Jonnie, who sat glaring at the teacher. "Are you satisfied?" she asked.

The teacher's eyes followed Thalia in distress, and then focused on Jonnie. "Are *you?* She came back to try to make it up! Why did you intrude? Why didn't you let her?"

"Leave her alone," said Jonnie. "You get paid for teaching, not sneaking to her mother. So why don't you just teach?"

44

"Who?" asked the teacher. "Who shall I teach? Thalia? Ada? Alicia? You, Jonnie? Shall I teach you? Did you read the poems I gave you?"

"I don't like poetry."

"Life can be a pathless wood where a branch cuts across your eyes open. What does that mean, Jonnie?"

"What *is* it with you and *poetry*?"

"What does it mean when the boy tries to subdue the birch tree by climbing the branches and he has to learn not to launch out too soon?" asked the teacher.

"You're crazy! You know that? *Look* at us! Do we need poetry!"

" 'They walk in darkness.' Robert Frost said that. 'Not of the woods and trees alone' . . . "

"What *is* it with teachers! This is a pregnant class! Everybody is stuck here if they want to pick up their welfare check! Tell me one person except you who likes poetry! Nobody needs it."

"Nobody in the Garden of Eden," said the teacher. "But once they ate the apple, they needed poetry to make them understand why they were cast out."

"Do me a favor," said Jonnie. "Tell Robert Frost to shove it."

Thalia sat in the corner, on the cold bathroom tiles, her bony knees drawn up, her face hidden in her crossed arms. "I'm gonna kill myself! You hear me? I'm gonna starve until I die!"

Antoinette settled her fat body down beside Thalia, resting her head on Thalia's shoulder. "Oh Thalia," she murmured.

"My momma says I can't do nuthin'. You call that blanket nuthin'?" She appealed to the room for justice. "You all seen

them felt butterflies I made for my baby. You call them butterflies nuthin'? With my own hands.'' She wept. "I ain't
stupid, like she says. Not with my baby! But she's all the time
standin' over me and I drop somethin'. They just look at me
sideways and I *drop* somethin'.''

"Don't tell me,'' said Ada. "They just come into the kitchen
and I *burn* something.''

"You're *lucky*,'' said Maryanne. "I don't even have a place
to drop or *burn*. My aunt has half my room and most of my
closet and they won't kick her out because she's mental.
They're shoving me on a studio couch.''

"Once,'' said Ada, "for *once* in my life, I would like to see a
whole TV program through without somebody turning my
station.''

"What kind of rights I have?'' asked Thalia. "Delonne is my
baby! *Who* suffered for him? *Who* got fourteen stitches? Did
she get fourteen stitches? So how come she got a right to take
my baby?''

The bathroom settled into heavy silence.

"I just want a place for my baby,'' said Thalia miserably. "I
can take care of him so fine, if they leave me be. Sometimes I
go into my momma's room at night and take him in bed with
me . . .''

"Just a room to myself,'' said Maryanne. "I only committed
one sin. I can't believe God wants me to go my whole life
without a room of my own.''

"Who doesn't need a place,'' said Jonnie. "Where you can
have your things around you and your own mail and nobody's big ears listening in on every phone call . . .''

"My own *phone*,'' moaned Maryanne. "I can't believe God
wants me to go my whole life without one toll call.''

"I would take care of him so fine,'' said Thalia. "I would
dress him so clean, and I would walk him to the market in his

carriage, and the people on the street they would stop me and they would say, 'Who is the momma of that fine baby?' "

"Where you can have a cup of hot cocoa," said Ada. "A place where you can watch your own programs for once without somebody turning on the news or something."

"With a marshmallow?" asked Antoinette, clasping her fat hands together. "Can we have a marshmallow in it?"

"Sure we can," said Jonnie. "And if somebody needed to come and stay with us, we would have a place for them. And if we wanted to stay up all night talking or watching TV, nobody would bitch at us."

"And if we didn't want to wash the dishes," said Maryanne, "we could leave the dishes. Dishes don't walk away, do they?"

"I could watch the babies . . . " Antoinette squinched up her face and urgently tugged at Jonnie's sleeve. "Can I watch the babies? *Please*, Jonnie!"

Alicia walked into the bathroom.

"Private . . ." said Jonnie.

Alicia stomped into a stall and slammed the door. "I ain't listening! I got to *go!*"

"Can I *come?*" pleaded Antoinette. *"Please . . ."* she wheezed, ". . . can I *come* . . ."

"Come where?" asked Jonnie.

"To our own *place!*"

They sat crocheting in silence, their fingers quietly weaving the soft bright colors. Ideas didn't come the way they did in cartoons, like bright electric lights over the head. They came in clouds, amorphous and filmy. They moved and swirled and coalesced and took shape. The yarn was soft and warm. Jonnie looked up at Ada, at Maryanne. They looked at each other, then back down to the little chains of stitches that bound up the thread and created the piece of soft blanket that would swaddle their babies. Thalia's fingers, long, thin, expert, flew through the yarn. She looked up at Jonnie, her eyes puffy, and then down again. Antoinette leaned against Jonnie's arm, holding the ball of yarn, handing out the thread as it was needed.

The house formed in her fantasy, along with the bright stitches. She saw Thalia on the porch of that house, rocking her baby. Ada's boyfriend working in the garden. Maryanne, like all the crazy sisters of all the TV families of her life, talking endlessly on the phone to Arthur. In the driveway Billy's old battered Ford. Upstairs, the sweet strings of Billy's guitar. From the kitchen, the warm odors of dinner cooking. On the steps, even Antoinette, the funny sister, sat with her open notebook.

"Put the yarn away now." The teacher urged them to straighten up. Mrs. Osley was waiting.

They folded the soft material and put the yarn away, glancing at each other, questioning, and getting excited.

"Stay a minute," the teacher said to Jonnie.

She didn't *have* a minute. Time was pressing. She began to see the picture clearly now. All of them together — a family — and in her own room Billy beside her, and the baby safe *inside* her, all of them joined in that same tight chain her needle had made of the soft yarn.

The teacher rarely lost her temper and suffered spasms of regret when she did. But if you sat through an apology, you ended up with a lecture. What Jonnie *didn't* need at this moment was another lecture.

"I didn't mean to be so sharp." The teacher was contrite.

"Just drop it. The bus is waiting."

"Let the bus wait."

"It's okay!" said Jonnie. "It's finished. You want me to apologize? I'm sorry! Just give your homework assignments and leave me alone. Will you, *please?*"

"What good does it do me to give you assignments when you all copy them out of the *World Book* and hand them back by rote? If this were a school for the deaf, you'd expect me to teach you sign language. Then why can't you let me help you to *see!*"

"I'm not *blind!*" said Jonnie.

"You're a six-month embryo," said the teacher. "Your eyes aren't even open yet."

"You *think* so!" she said. "It really bugs you, doesn't it, that nobody gives a damn about your poetry! Get it through your head that I don't need advice! I need a house for my baby. Now if you can get me that, I'll listen!"

"That's what I'm trying to tell you, Jonnie! What did Robert Frost mean when he said that home was a place where, when you had to go there, they had to take you in? Think of what home means to you and to your baby!"

"You think I haven't!" she screamed. "Home? Don't ask Robert Frost about home! Because Robert Frost wasn't almost seven months pregnant, was he! And alone! And stuck in a house where no one wants him! I *know* what home is!" A warm flush came to her face. Suddenly, and with such clarity that she could touch him, her father's image came to her. The hot flush spread to her neck and to her stomach. Her worlds were in collision. She tried to block the teacher out, to erase this dumb sterile obsolete nothing of a room. She wanted them to shut up. She wanted no more to talk to this teacher than to any of them who stood on the other side of the glass keeping her from what was rightly hers, but the words came hot, like lava, unbidden, from the source. The heat boiled in her and the anger simmered and poured between the cracks. "I know what home is. It's a place where they don't push at you and they don't shove at you. It's a place where if your eye falls on something, it's a flower or a rock or a butterfly, and when you open the curtains in the morning, the sun comes in soft and they *listen* soft." Her father's voice came to her in a rush of wings. *Poor Jonnie.* The voice became a feeling. She wanted to hold that feeling, to have it, to feel it again. But it was gone. She was standing alone in the schoolroom, yelling at a *teacher!* She moaned in embarrassment.

"Jonnie," said the teacher, "I understand. It's all right."

"Do you?" she sputtered. "Do you really? You just love to listen in and pry out our personal secrets, don't you! And then you go home and sit around drinking coffee and talk about us and cluck your tongues at how awful things are for the *poor girls!* You and your big sympathy act!"

"It's not true!" protested the teacher.

"Isn't it? You just hate when we listen to soap operas because they're so junky. But in secret, *we're* your soap opera, aren't we! Liars! You're all liars!" She ran for the door.

The teacher's voice followed after her. "Jonnie . . ."

"Liars and cheats!"

The bus was waiting for her. She pulled herself aboard. "Just take all day!" called Mrs. Osley. "Take your own sweet time! I've got a class of crippled children waiting to go to the zoo!"

Thalia and Maryanne waved to her from the back seat. The bus lurched forward.

"Sit right!" called Mrs. Osley. "If you think you're going to sit crooked and fall down and collect the insurance, you've got another think coming."

They saw that something awful had happened. They crowded around her to give comfort. "What do they *want*

50

from us?" asked Ada. "They already wrecked the Indians. What *else* do they want?"

"Nobody understands, except the Virgin," said Maryanne, "so if *she* isn't mad, why is *every*body?"

"They see you're nobody, so they yell at you," said Thalia. "Why don't they be nice to you if you're lonesome? But you're nobody, so they yell."

"*Who's* nobody!" said Jonnie. "We're sisters, aren't we? That's somebody! We came in on the same day! We got pregnant in the same week! That's something, isn't it! It *means* something! It's *for* something!"

"It was a weird thing," said Ada. "Who knows . . ."

"There *has* to be a reason for things," said Maryanne. "Things have to happen for something. Otherwise, ·what good is sin?"

"I'm a *late* sister," said Thalia, holding back the way she always did when she was afraid she wasn't going to get a thing. "I suffered to be a sister, so I'm titled! Black is beautiful!"

It came to her suddenly, all at once, that what happened happened for something! She had not been told what yet, but when they were ready, they would tell her. "We suffered!" she whooped. "We're 'titled!" she laughed. She hugged Thalia. They all hugged each other. It was funny . . . it was solemn . . . it was a vow.

The whole bus turned to watch them. "Take care what you're doing back there!" called Mrs. Osley.

"*Take care*," mimicked Jonnie in Mrs. Osley's voice. "Take care you don't fall down and kill yourself and try to collect the insurance!" She slammed the side of the pregnant bus with her fist. "Let *every*body shove it! We're a family! Let's get ourselves a house!"

51

3

Loveliest of Trees, the Cherry Now

Jonnie hung up the phone quietly and hurried toward her room. But somebody's big ears had heard. Her mother rushed into the hallway. "What's wrong? Who's calling this early?"

"Nobody." She closed her bedroom door and started to dress. But her mother pushed in after her, carping at her. "Who was it? Where are you going this early? It's too early for the school bus . . ." It dawned on her mother slowly. "It's not *him* again! Not Billy again! You're not getting mixed up with that Billy again!"

She brushed her hair vigorously to smooth it down.

"He came back to town and he phoned you, didn't he! After everything he did to you, he phoned you and you're running back to him!"

"Leave me alone!" she said. "I know what I'm doing!" She bent with effort to retrieve a shoe from under the bed. She was getting so clumsy.

"Haven't you learned your lesson with that beach bum? You made one mistake! I can understand one mistake! But how can you make two!"

52

"Right," she said. "But isn't it funny that everybody I happen to like turns out to be a bum?"

"Believe me, Jonnie, I know Billy Veller! Leave Billy Veller alone!"

"You called my father a bum," she said.

Her mother sat on the edge of the bed, holding her robe around her. ". . . I didn't."

"Didn't you?"

When they were together in a room, all the air went out of it. You couldn't breathe. "That was between me and your father. It had nothing to do with you."

"Didn't it?" she asked.

Her mother floundered, looking for arguments, searching for something, anything that would pop her balloon. "Leave him alone. He's too old for you."

"He's not too old. Abel is older than you are."

"Abel! What has Abel got to do with it? I'm not going to let you get mixed up with Billy Veller again! I'm still your mother, Jonnie! I forbid you to see him again! I won't permit it. You're still under age!"

"Don't scream at me," said Jonnie. "Not anymore. I'm not your slave anymore. When I got pregnant, I became emancipated. So there's nothing you can do about it, is there."

"Listen to me!" Her mother's voice echoed after her as she left the house. "Leave him alone! *Jonnie* . . ."

Billy sprinted across the patch of grass and caught the limb of the tree, chinned himself, fell into a somersault, rolled toward her where she sat on the grass and lay with his head on her lap, what was *left* of her lap with the baby growing the way it was, and laughed up at her. "My luck is changing. Jonnie brought me good luck!"

She tried to take his hand and place it on her stomach.

53

"Feel the baby move."

"Listen," he said, excited about something, "after I left you last night, I met these two guys . . ."

"It's the baby. The baby is bringing you luck."

"*Listen* to me. These guys just came back from Alaska. Working on some kind of pipeline. There's a job I can get in Alaska! No experience! Just a strong arm . . ."

"Alaska!"

"Listen to me! You know what you can make on that job? A thousand a week! A thousand!"

"*Alaska?*"

He must have seen the dismay on her face. "Will you listen for a second? It's cold as hell up there! You couldn't stand it for very long. You'd freeze your butt off. But they take you no experience — nothing. If you could hold out a month or six weeks, you'd be set. So what do you think?"

She understood what he was saying! He was leaving her again! "No!" She felt the panic rise in her. "You promised to stay until the baby came!"

"This is a thousand a *week*, honey!"

"You're crazy! Who pays a thousand a week for anything!"

"I *told* you! You're not listening to me! It's in Alaska! It's freezing cold up there! But if you could hold out for a month . . ."

She wanted to listen to him! But she couldn't understand what he was saying! And her mother's voice nagged at her. *He ran out on you once . . .* "What about the baby! You promised!"

He sat up in frustration. "Okay. How long until it comes? How many weeks?"

She was trying to see his side of it, to give him equal time with her mother's carping voice. "I don't know exactly . . . maybe eight or nine."

54

"Eight or nine! Do you know how cold it's going to be up there in eight or nine weeks?"

She buried her face in his chest. "You promised."

He pulled her away so that she had to look at him. "When you phoned me, I came. I drove all night to get here because I heard how scared you were, and I want to help you with the baby. But I'm flat! I had to sleep in the car last night! Now I've got a chance to put a buck in my pocket. And you want me to wait until its freezing cold up there? Okay, Jonnie. You call it."

"I'm trying to *tell* you!" she insisted. "We're getting a house! Four of us! We're pooling our welfare and getting a house!"

"House? I don't need a house! I need a buck in my pocket!" He lay back and closed his eyes. "When . . . when are you getting a house?"

"Soon. We're starting to look today."

"Then you want me to sleep in the car until you find it?"

She searched his face for the truth of it. She needed to see the truth in his eyes. So she took a terrible risk. "Would you have come back?" she blurted out. "If I hadn't called you."

He held her as he spoke. He put his hand to her face and touched her cheek while he answered her. And she held her baby and prayed.

"I'm going to tell how it was, Jonnie. I'm telling you the way it really was. When I met you, I liked you. You were a good kid. A nice kid. You made me laugh. I had a good time with you last summer. But that was it. I came back because you were in a fix. I know what it is to be in a fix, Jonnie. The way it is with me, I've been drifting all my life. People are pretty rotten all in all. You can't trust anybody to love you. People let you down. But something happened when I came back. You're such a funny kid, Jonnie. And I think I trust *you*.

55

When somebody loves you, and you trust they love you, it changes your luck. Well, my luck is changing! I feel it in my bones. You don't know me, honey. You don't know what I dream or what I want. I have big dreams! And I decided to stick with you. If I say I'll stick, then I'll stick. And I expect you to stick with me."

"I'll stick!" she said fervently. "I'll never let you down."

"So I'm going to San Diego with these guys and find out more about the deal. Okay?"

What else could she say but okay.

Now she had San Diego to worry about.

His eyes were already on something far away. "A couple of thousand, Jonnie. Four, maybe five, if I can stick it out, and then we can leave this town, see where the wind blows."

"Touch the baby," she begged him. "For luck."

"You're my good-luck-Jonnie," he said. "I'll bring you something from San Diego."

The pregnant bus was late. She was dying for something to eat — something — anything — a Coke — a candy bar. While she waited on the corner for the market to open, she talked it over with her baby. Her mother's voice accused. She defended. Her baby listened in judgment. If he were running out on her, why would he have bothered to tell her? Alaska meant gone again, but it also meant coming back! He had been honest to tell her he didn't love her the first time, but he loved her now. And this time the coming back for her wiped out the first time. That was logic. Her baby turned in agreement, but moved again under her heart to remind her. *Don't worry*, she chided her baby. *I'm not forgetting you.*

She watched the produce man hefting boxes of fruit to put out on the stands. She saw him uncrating the cartons of cherries. Cherries? This late in the season? Where did they get cherries from now that the season was over? Probably cost a fortune. But she needed cherries. She had suffered, hadn't she? She deserved them. And so she bought cherries. Big fat globes of cherries that shone like jewels. She quickly recited again the litany of her anguishes and trials, the enormity of the injustices perpetrated against her. It was only fitting that she should console herself with cherries.

They sank their teeth into them, squeezed out the sweet juice, sucked the comforting hard knots of seeds, clicked them between their teeth and spit them into the aisle of Mrs. Osley's bus.

"I told my mother," said Maryanne, holding a cherry in the pouch of her cheek before she chewed on it, "about the house and all. She cried all night."

Ada spit a seed out the window. "Your mother cries all night over 'As the World Turns.' It's your father I'm worried about. When she got pregnant, they had to fly her sister down from Sacramento to keep him from killing her."

"They told him it was God's judgment on him," said Maryanne, "on account of his drinking. My mother says the house is a sin because Arthur might be in it. Why is it a sin if it feels good? And if they burn you or nail you up or something, that's good for your immortal soul?" She crossed herself.

"It's *him* I'm worried about," said Ada, taking a cherry, "more than me, even. If they let him off and I don't have a place to keep an eye on him, he's liable to go back on the streets again."

"Who's letting *who* off?" asked Alicia from across the aisle. "Once they get a Chicano or an Indian, they don't *ever* let him off."

"It's okay." Ada grinned broadly, which she rarely did. "He finally found himself a public defender who's crazy about Chief Dan George. My boyfriend is teaching him war dances."

"How does he know war dances," asked Alicia, "if he's never been to Dakota?"

Ada chomped so hard on cherries that the juice ran down her mouth as she grinned. "Doesn't. Jumps around and makes noises. Lawyer doesn't know the difference." But the smile faded and she wiped her mouth with her hand and settled back to her usual Ada face. "I went to see him yesterday. He's going crazy locked up in there. In front of the other guys, he yells at me like a big shot. Then he gets me alone, and he cries like a baby. He's scared, Jonnie."

The bus groaned to a stop and Thalia, long-legged and skinny, swung aboard and stomped down the aisle. She fell into a seat, slumped disconsolate, keeping her own counsel. They offered her a cherry. She took it and sucked on it. "Laughed at me," she said. "Said I'm a fool. Nobody is gonna rent no house to no fool, especially if she's a black fool. Color prejudice," she accused wanly.

"Why are you listening to liars?" asked Jonnie.

Thalia spit a seed into her hand. "What if we don't get it? It hurts my heart to think about it. What if we don't?"

The what-if's descended.

"What if they don't rent houses to people like us?"

"What if my social worker finds out?"

"I'm sick of what-ifs," said Jonnie. "You can what-if the whole thing to death. What if there's an earthquake tomorrow and L.A. falls into the *ocean* or something?"

The whole bus knocked on that one.

"I had a friend who got a house," said Alicia. "In the middle of the night, somebody put a gas hose to her keyhole and shot in gas and knocked them all out and stole their color TV and their toaster oven."

"Watch where you're throwing those cherry pips!" warned Mrs. Osley. "If you think you're going to slip on a cherry pip and collect the insurance, you've got another think coming!"

They each spit a cherry seed into the aisle.

"What I'd like to know," complained Mrs. Osley over the sound of traffic, "what I'd like to know is how girls on welfare can afford cherries when I can't even afford cherries."

"Poor Mrs. Osley," said somebody.

"She can't afford cherries," said somebody.

"That's why they give her the pips!"

"No appreciation!" called Mrs. Osley. "When I was a girl, nobody gave me a free ride on a bus and a welfare check for having a baby!"

"When you was a girl!" they all roared, "they still had horses!"

The whole class was cracking up over the film. It was embarrassing to see the old lady doctor demonstrate how to breast-feed your baby on a *huge*-breasted woman. The girls couldn't subdue their laughter.

"She look like a cow," said somebody.

"I ain't feedin my baby with my titties," said somebody. "My boyfriend, he would *kill* me."

The nurse switched off the projector and turned on the lights. "Who said titties? *Who* in this class is calling breasts *titties!*"

"Let's do English or something," said Alicia. "I don't like no movies about the nasties."

"Since *when* are breasts nasty? And since *when* is *sex* nasty?"

"Shoo," said somebody. "She don't know my boyfriend."

"Then explain it to me," said the nurse. "When is sex nasty? If you're *not* married? If you're married, is sex nasty? If you *enjoy* it, is sex nasty?"

"If you're not, it's nasty," said Alicia. "Sometimes if you *are*, it's nasty. And who enjoys it?"

"Then why *do* it?"

"*They* want . . ." said Alicia.

"And *they* don't like you to use the breast to feed your baby? Since when do *they* have more control over your bodies then *you* do?"

"That's the way they do," said somebody.

"Well if *they* don't understand that it's your body and your baby, that you're emancipated women, go get yourself another boyfriend! Somebody who's considerate and understanding."

"My sister ought to get a new boyfriend," said Alicia. "But she's afraid she won't find one on account of her bad skin. She wrote to *Dearabby*. And *Dearabby* told her to get a skin peel. You know what a skin peel costs? It's easier to keep the boyfriend."

"But you have to understand that sex related to love is not nasty! If you feel your body is nasty or any body functions are nasty, then how will your baby learn to feel good about itself? Do you understand me?"

Nobody was interested in understanding her.

"What I'm trying to say is that if you don't *want* to, *don't!* You're free women!"

"Tell *them!*" said somebody.

"Please," said the nurse, "I'm explaining it badly. This time, ask questions. This time, *please* ask questions."

Alicia raised her hand. "I heard once about a man who did

the nasties with a monkey and the baby came out half a man and half a monkey."

"No!" said the nurse. "Not true!"

"I heard about a lady who did it with a dog or a horse or something. In a motel room," said somebody.

"How do they get a horse in a motel room?" asked somebody.

"I'm talking about sex as a manifestation of love, as it relates to your babies. Do you understand *love?*"

"Never say love," said somebody. "You say *love*, they get too sure of themself."

The nurse gave up and started to rewind the film. "Then explain something else to me. With all your expenses, with all the things you have to buy out of those checks which are pitifully small, how can you afford *cherries* out of season?"

" 'Loveliest of trees,' " said the teacher, " 'the cherry now is hung with white along the bough.' A. E. Housman said that."

"I thought this was Consumer Ed," said Ada, sucking a cherry.

"What I'm trying to say," said the teacher, "is that the cherry has always been the subject of aesthetic appreciation. The Oriental artist, his fragile cherry blossoms . . . a favorite lullaby of mine which I'm going to play for you as soon as I restring my guitar is 'I Gave My Love a Cherry.' What I mean to say is that I understand the joys of cherries out of season. There are many wonderful things that evoke our immediate desire and beg for gratification."

"The cherries really bug her, *don't* they," said Jonnie.

"*Stop* that," said the teacher, "and *listen*. Let's say that you want something big, something that requires more money than you have in pocket. A washing machine, for instance. So you forgo cherries out of season and you put aside X dollars toward a washing machine."

Ada sucked a cherry. "You'd have to give up cherries for the rest of your life. It's easier to go to the launderette."

"I gave *my* love a cherry," said Alicia, "and look what it got me. He took me to Pismo Beach and said we were getting married. Then when we got home, he said we were getting a divorce. You can get divorced from a person, but you can't get divorced from a baby. He'll find out."

Antoinette shoved herself in beside Jonnie at the Consumer Ed table and tugged at Jonnie's arm. She squinched the way she did when she wanted something and couldn't put together the words. "I *want* . . ." she said finally.

"Want what?" asked the teacher. "You too, Antoinette? Do you want to buy cherries out of season?"

"Want to watch the *babies*," she whispered, "at our *house*."

"*What* house?" asked the teacher.

Jonnie poked Antoinette to make her shut up. Antoinette pulled away, offended, then leaned back toward Jonnie for solace. "I *want* to . . ." she wheezed, ". . . like the other children . . ."

"It kills him to have to do it," said Ada. "It's such a sweet little Chevy convertible. But he's nervous and he has to have money for smokes. To bribe the guards with. He'll die stuck in there if he can't smoke. So anybody want to chip in twenty-five bucks apiece for a sweet little sixty-one Chevy? We'll need a car if we're looking for a house."

"Put me in," said Thalia anxiously. "Hurry and get it. She's feedin' my baby and he's startin' to look up in *her* face. *Please.* Before he learns *her* face and not me!"

*

62

"You want to see James Bond again or *Jaws* again?" They walked against the wind toward Baskin-Robbins.

"James Bond," said Maryanne. "I can't stand that dead face in the boat."

"Why not?" asked Ada. "You've got plenty of practice with Arthur."

"Don't *talk* like that," she begged. "He's got good qualities."

"Name one," said Ada.

They all knocked on a packing crate, because the house needed all the luck it could get. "How does knocking bring luck?" Jonnie asked. It was a blasphemous question. She sensed the Fates frowning their displeasure. She knocked again, with more humility.

"Let him come to you this time," said Jonnie. "Play it cool. See what he does."

"Just don't beg," said Ada. "I hate to see anybody beg someone like Arthur."

He sauntered by, a bent stick in a school sweater.

"Boy," said Ada. "What a zero. Beats me how the white man ever conquered the Indians."

"Don't talk him down," said Maryanne. "Nobody knows him like I do."

Arthur offered Maryanne first bite of the cone. "Want to go to a show on Friday night?"

Maryanne burst into tears, leaned over and hugged him in gratitude. "What time will you come? I'll get dressed up."

"Do something with your hair," he said. "It looks terrible."

She kissed the hand that held the cone.

"Hey — " he said offhandedly, as if he just remembered something. "Hey, you know those notes I sent you back in

63

school? My mother is really giving me a hard time about those notes."

Maryanne flushed red in the cheeks and down her neck. "How does your mother *know!*"

"She's got this thing in her head about those letters. She'll send me to diving school in San Diego if I get them back."

"That's it," said Ada. "Let's go."

They pulled Maryanne out of her chair.

"Let me stay!" she protested. "He's taking me *out* on Friday!"

They dragged her away from the table. "She isn't giving any letters back," said Ada. "My boyfriend happens to know a very smart lawyer. Don't marry her. See what happens."

"Who said I wouldn't marry her!"

"He *will!*" cried Maryanne. She tried to get back to him. "You heard him! He says he *will!*"

"Marry her first. Then the letters."

"The hell with the letters!" said Arthur desperately. "Let my mother have the letters! What does everybody *want* from me! My mother wants me to dump her! *She* wants to keep the baby! I haven't got a job even! *I* want to learn to be a diver! Doesn't anybody care what *I* want! If Maryanne gives back the letters, my mother sends me to diving school and I can afford to get married! Give me a break, Maryanne!"

"Talk to her on Friday," said Ada.

"What time!" called Maryanne as they dragged her out.

"Meet me in front of the Fox at eight!"

"She's not meeting you anyplace!" called Jonnie. "Pick her up!"

"My mother would kill me!"

"Some loss," said Ada.

*

64

They pushed her along the Mall. She tried to turn back but they linked arms and pulled her along. She yielded finally. "Who has a hair dryer? I have to do something about my hair."

"Let Arthur do something about his face," said Ada. "So do we want to see *Great Gatsby* again or *Dog Day Afternoon* again?"

"*Gatsby*," said Jonnie. She loved the way Fate had torn the lovers apart and how they met again and fell in love again after all those sad years.

"What good was it?" asked Ada. "They shoot him in the end and nobody comes to the funeral. And I can't stand where Al Pacino is a fag in *Dog Day*. It's such a waste."

"Let's go see *The Sting* again," said Maryanne. "At least somebody lives in that one. You have to have somebody living once in a while."

They walked into Thrifty to check the *Examiner* horoscope. Ada had to be careful with her superiors, especially in office matters. Maryanne had to attend to matters of personal urgency, especially in the A.M. and avoid investments. Jonnie was to expect an important visit from a stranger. They all knocked the wooden paper rack for luck.

"Who hears when you knock wood?" asked Jonnie again. She was annoyed that it bothered her.

"One of these days," said Ada, "they're going to make a movie with Robert Redford and James Caan and Paul Newman and Al Pacino, all at the same time. That day I'll sit in the movies forever." The thought was delicious. They stopped at a bakery and bought a bag of sugar doughnuts and went to see the show.

*

"Who?" screamed her mother. "Who in their right mind is going to rent a house to four pregnant children?"

"You'll see." She finished her milk and headed for the bedroom.

"Jonnie, use what's left of your sense . . ."

"Just wait." she said.

"Is this *his* idea? Did *he* put you up to it?"

She slammed the bedroom door.

"What will you do by yourself? When the baby comes!"

"I happen to have friends."

"He dumped you once, Jonnie. He'll dump you again."

She put her hands over her ears. "You're always yelling that if it weren't for me, you could be doing this and that! Leave me alone! Go do it!"

Her mother rattled the door handle, but didn't try to open the door. "I never said that."

"Not much! I wish I had the tape."

"I didn't mean it that way."

She heard her mother's steps retreating finally. She turned on her lamp and made herself a little nest of blankets in her bed. She curled in the center and visited with her baby. She had saved a cherry seed for sucking, and she sucked it now, rocking her baby and herself. She sorted out things she was trying to understand. That her baby was like a growing seed inside her, not a separate thing to be kept or given away, like an object, but part of her own *self*. She leaned toward her stomach. "Warm in there?" Her baby turned in languid comfort. Billy was still too far from the baby to understand that she and the baby were an entity, that the baby was the luck part of her, that her luck had been missing and had been restored with the baby. Her baby stretched, touching the boundaries of its little warm home, curled and slept again.

She was bringing Billy luck. When was it decided, she wondered, who had luck and who didn't? Why did some people
have houses and fathers without having to fight for them, or
beg for them — like Maryanne, who was begging for something not even worthy of her. If you questioned the Fates,
would you in a way be tempting them to take *away* your luck?
She hugged and rocked her baby. "I love you," she said. "Do
you love me?" Why was everybody so up-tight about the
baby when the baby was the luckiest thing that ever happened to her?

4

Slimy Heads and Things
That Go Bump in the Night

THE COUNSELOR'S NAME was Duquette. Don Duquette. So they all called him Donald Duck and they quacked when they went into the office to talk over their credits or their transfers, or to get advice. She had no use for counselors. All she needed was a school counselor giving her advice on something he knew nothing about.

"Into the office. He's waiting for you."

"Leave me alone," said Jonnie. "I don't need a counselor."

"Then go in there and *sit* for fifteen minutes."

She could have stared the teacher down. She could have made a thing of it. But she had too much on her mind. It wasn't worth the hassle.

The counselor, his thin shoulders, his long neck, his shock of wiry hair, sat, as usual, shuffling papers. She walked in reluctantly and fell into a chair. "Quack," she said.

"My name is Duquette," he said. "Not duck. If anybody waddles around this classroom, it's not me. But you see how tactful I am not to mention it? So what's new, Jonnie? I'm glad to see you."

"Why?" she asked.

"Because you're my favorite reading material. The most interesting records in town. You go up and down like storm warnings on a barometer. You've taken classes and failed classes and passed classes without rhyme or reason. What am I going to do with you?"

"Nothing," she said. "Don't do anything with me."

He leaned back in his chair, cocked his head to one side like a pigeon and looked at her. "Okay. So ask me some other questions."

"*What* other questions?"

"How should I know what other questions? What's on your mind? Cooking? Fashions? Real estate? You want me to cast your horoscope or interpret your dreams?"

"You're crazy," she said. "What do you know about dreams?"

"Ask me and find out."

She shrugged. He was a comedian. "If you dream you're falling and you hit the ground before you wake up, you die, right?"

"Wrong."

"Since when?" she asked.

"Since always. People always dream they're falling, but they never die from it."

"You sure about that?"

"About some things, no. About that, yes. Medically proved."

She leaned closer. "If you dream you're running naked in the street and people are standing around and watching, does that make you weird or what?"

"Dreams never make you weird. If everybody who dreamed he was running around naked were weird, we'd all be in trouble. We all have the same kinds of dreams, being human. Most of us dream the same dream symbols. See how much I know? Ask me more."

"Are you serious or are you kidding?" she said.

"When am I ever kidding?"

"Then what does it mean if you dream you're lost in an ugly house and all the doors are open but nobody is in the house and suddenly you're frightened?"

"That you have to answer for yourself. Dreams are little messengers . . . from inside. We always know the meaning, but we have to piece the parts together like a puzzle. So, you think about it and tell me. What does it mean to *you* to be lost in an ugly house and all the doors are open but nobody is in the house and suddenly you get frightened?"

"You're weird, you know that? If I knew what it meant, I wouldn't ask you. If you know so much about dreams, do you know about luck?"

"No such thing as luck."

"You're nuts!" she said.

"Probably, but there's no such thing as luck."

"Everybody knows about luck, what happens or doesn't happen to you."

"What happens or doesn't happen to people, they make happen themselves. They make their own luck."

"You're *crazy!* If everybody made their own luck, they'd all make good luck. We'd all be millionaires."

"There's one hitch," said Donald Duck. "It depends on how you feel about yourself. If you like yourself well enough, you make yourself good luck. Every time you make a decision or a choice, you choose right because you're such a nice guy,

why *shouldn't* you deserve all that good luck. But if you're
angry with yourself or disappointed, or if you don't *like* yourself, you write yourself a mess of misery."

"That's a lie!"

"Blasphemy to Walt Disney. Donald Ducks don't lie."

"But if somebody has natural bad luck, and you love them
with *true* love, you can change their luck."

"If it's true love, as you say, maybe you can give somebody
more confidence to love themselves, Jonnie. But the only luck
you can change is your own."

"That's *stupid!* When does it get decided if you like yourself
or not?"

He tapped her stomach. "In there. When your baby is
born. After it's born. If you want the baby, if you've learned
how to love the baby, it will have all the luck it needs."

"You're crazy! Who has to learn about love?"

"You'd be surprised how many people. Love is very tricky.
It comes in disguises, like Shakespeare's villains. You have to
listen carefully to your body to find out whether or not you've
learned how to love."

"Are you trying to tell me that I don't love my *baby!*"

"That's not what I said. You tell me. How does it make you
feel to love your baby?"

"Wonderful, that's how it makes me feel. Good. It makes
me warm, and happy."

"How does it make you feel to love your baby's father?"

"That," she said acidly, "is a different kind of love, which
you wouldn't understand."

"I've got news for you," said Donald Duck. "Love is a great
equalizer, a great democratizer. Even an odd duck can feel
the same love as Robert Redford. How does it make you feel
to love your baby's father?"

Counselors were pitiful. "You wouldn't understand how a real woman feels about a real man."

"Pardon *me*," he said, "you mean a *real* woman and a *real* man — the kind of love that's full of pain and anxiety, where it hurts so much and it makes you cry, but if you're a *real* woman longing for a *real* man, it's worth it."

"That's right!" she said. "And if you think that just because we're not as old as you are . . ."

"That's not love!" said Donald Duck. "That's a bellyache. Love should always make you feel good. Love should make you laugh, it should make you grow, the way you're growing that baby. You understand me?"

She stood up and gave him a thanks-for-nothing smile. "Quack, quack!" she said.

"You amaze me," said the counselor.

"Why? Because I'm the only one with guts enough to tell you how I feel?"

"No. Because you're the first customer who's understood what I've said."

"*Who* understood? I forgot it already."

"Can you forget the left eye of a donkey?" he said.

"You're bananas," she said.

"So what's wrong with bananas? Come again, any time. The price is right."

She quacked and waddled back to her seat.

"All dreams," said the teacher, "all hopes, all aspirations begin in fantasy. But we have to know the difference between the kind of fantasy that's a fairy tale and the kind of fantasy that builds a life. The trouble with your educations is that you were all brought up on stories like "A Visit to the Post Office" and "Farmer Small." You never had the wild and wonderful fairy tales, full of witches and ogres, princesses and frogs, full of rich symbolism . . ."

"We have Frankenstein," said Alicia, "and Son of . . ."

"I mean the wonderful little moralities, the allegories that I hope you'll tell to your own children."

" 'Sesame Street,' " said somebody. "I watch it myself."

". . . and since nobody is doing the poetry, I'm starting a unit on fairy tales and the first story I'd like to tell you is 'The Slimy Head in the Pond.' "

Antoinette whispered and drew closer to Jonnie.

"It's make-believe," said the teacher. "It's not real, but it has real meaning. Once upon a time, there were three sisters, two cruel and selfish sisters and one sweet kind sister . . ."

"That's the way in families," said somebody.

". . . and the cruel sisters were lazy and they made the kind sister go down to the pond to wash the clothes."

"Didn't they have a launderette in their building?" asked somebody.

"These were olden times, before washing machines. They had to wash their clothes in a pond."

"In cold water?" asked somebody.

"They have Cold Water Tide," said somebody.

". . . *so*, as she was washing the clothes, suddenly, up out of the pond, rose an ugly slimy head . . ."

"I saw it in a Japanese movie," said somebody.

"I hate dirty old men," said Alicia. "We got one on our block."

". . . and *so* the slimy head spoke to the kind sister. 'Little sister, little sister, comb my hair . . .' "

"He followed me down the street," said Alicia, "in a trench coat."

73

". . . and *so* the kind sister took her own little comb and combed the tangled, matted hair . . ."

"Shoo," said Thalia, "I ain't combin' nobody's dirty hair. Don't care what they promise."

". . . and then the slimy head said, 'Little sister, little sister, will you wash my face . . .' "

"I hope she's watching her purse," said Alicia. "That's a good way to get yourself mugged."

". . . and so she washed his face with her own handkerchief, and then the slimy head said, 'Little sister, little sister, will you kiss me?' "

"You should never kiss on a first date," said somebody, "especially a weirdo."

"The point," said the teacher, "is that the good sister didn't care what he looked like. She was kind and giving, and he rewarded her by making pearls and diamonds fall from her lips when she spoke."

"I had a friend," said Alicia, "she choked on a piece of steak in a restaurant. You could *choke* on a pearl."

"You can't take it too literally," said the teacher. "What does it mean to have diamonds fall from your lips?"

"You can cut your mouth on a diamond," said Alicia. "My sister's boyfriend uses diamonds to cut glass."

"And *so*," said the teacher, "when the cruel sisters saw the pearls and diamonds, they demanded to know where the good sister got them, and they went down to the pond, and the slimy head rose out of the water . . ."

"Probably was a whole man," said Alicia, "and he just stuck out his head. They got some line."

". . . but the selfish and cruel sisters wouldn't wash his face or comb his hair because he was so ugly . . ."

"First they ask you to wash their face," said Alicia, "and

then they want you to comb their hair, and then you *know* what. You can't trust no men."

". . . and out of the mouths of the ugly sisters came toads and snakes," said the teacher.

"I saw it in a Japanese movie," said somebody. "This head came out of a pond and ate New York."

The teacher closed her book. "Would you rather hear the story of Rose White and Rose Red and the prince who turned into a bear?"

"You start washing their faces and stuff," said Alicia, "and they turn into something all right."

"So, what's the meaning of the story?" asked the teacher. "What's the allegory? What does it mean to have pearls and diamonds falling from her lips, and toads."

Antoinette squinched up her face and raised her hand tentatively.

"Yes, Antoinette."

Antoinette blushed, leaned into Jonnie's arm. "*I* would . . ." she whispered. She buried her face in embarrassment.

"You would what?" asked the teacher.

"Wash his *face* . . ." she wheezed.

"*Would* you," said the teacher, "And why would you, Antoinette?"

She peered out of the haven of Jonnie's arm. "He's nice," she whispered. "He calls me 'Little sister . . .' "

"Then pearls and diamonds will fall from your lips."

Antoinette tugged in pleasure at a lank lock of hair. "I get to watch the babies," she said breathlessly.

"Where?" asked the teacher.

Jonnie poked her to shut up.

She drew away. "I *want* to . . ."

"Want to what?" asked the teacher.

75

She looked at Jonnie, hurt at the rebuff, but leaned toward her, burying her face in Jonnie's arm. ". . . be a little sister."

They all sat around eating and talking and enjoying the best part of the school day. "Weird heads and that," said Ada. "I hope we don't get a house like the house in *The Haunting*, where the walls bulge in the middle of the night. Gives me the creeps."

"You believe in ghosts?" asked Maryanne.

"You?" asked Ada.

"I believe in the Holy Ghost," said Maryanne, "but he doesn't make the walls bulge."

"There's a difference between ghosts and spirits," said Ada.

"I seen one," said Thalia.

"Where?" asked Jonnie. The skin at the back of her neck prickled.

"In my room. In the dark. Okay with you if I use a night light?"

"Okay by me," said Ada. "They make fun of me at home if I use it. But if it's dark and I wake up, the walls bulge."

"I hate 'Now I lay me . . .' " said Maryanne. " 'If I should *die* before I wake.' I trust God and everything, but it sounds like an invitation."

It was making her nervous, all this ghost talk. Her own ghosts lived in the closet. Not that she believed it, really. But on certain nights she kept her head down under the covers a lot. Until she could touch wood.

She took the rest of her sandwich and walked over to the English table where the teacher still sat, reading her own fairy tales. "Don't you ever give up?"

"Not when I'm stalking the enemy."

76

"What *enemy.*"

The teacher went back to reading *Bluebeard*. Jonnie went back to a heated discussion on the validity of ghosts. *Bluebeard!* Teachers in general were crazy. They lived in a separate alien world. That's why she rarely bothered to learn their names.

5

Still No Room at the Inn

THEY CHUGGED DOWN the boulevard in the little Chevy coupe with the top down. The car coughed, hesitated, coughed again, sputtered its exhaust a couple of times, sending up spumes of gray smoke, and then spurted forward. "Just has to warm up," called Ada.

"I'm *freezing* back here!" called Maryanne over the noise of traffic. "Can we get the top up?"

"He was going to fix the top," called Ada, "as soon as he fixed the door handle." She hit a horn at a pedestrian in the crosswalk. "Who has right of way?"

Jonnie turned to get a good look at Maryanne. "What did you do to your face?" Maryanne had painted a red slash of lipstick across her mouth.

"Made myself up to look older."

"She looks like she's bleeding," called Ada. "I tied up my braids, but they're too tight. They're giving me a headache." She made a left turn from the outside lane. Horns blasted at her. "Sorry about that!" she called. She swerved to the curb

78

and turned off the key. The little Chevy continued to cough, shudder, shake, finally died. "Some power!" she said. She hit the horn a couple of times.

Thalia waved to them from an upstairs window where she sat crying, her face pressed against the glass. Thalia's mother marched out of the front door, drying her hands on her apron.

"Let's go," said Maryanne. "What I don't need today is another mother."

Thalia's mother approached the car critically, circled it in disapproval. "This the piece of junk you all threw away twenty-five hard dollars on?"

"Okay if Thalia comes with us?" asked Ada.

"Who got the pink slip?" asked the mother.

"What's a pink slip?" asked Ada.

The mother hit the side of the car with the flat of her hand. "Fools! Bunch of fools! Thalia's got work to do. She's got pots to wash, and laundry. And if you had the sense you were born with, you'd go home and learn how to take care of a house before you start gettin' one. Thalia's got to understand what this world is, and what's in it."

Ada started the motor.

"Let her get herself a little job and leave that baby to somebody who can take care of it! No fool can't take care of no baby."

The motor caught. The car leaped forward.

"You can't eat butterflies!" the mother called after them.

The house had been so rich in their fantasies, so available, so perfect, that the real house looked oddly formal, darkly oppressive. They sat in the car looking at it.

"I'll wait here," said Ada. "I forgot to change my tennis

shoes. I feel funny going in a place like that in tennis shoes."

It wasn't the tennis shoes and they all knew it. It was asking and expecting. It was eyes and glances and tones, and leaving the protection of familiar places vulnerable to the pot shots of the outside world. Even the car was security. They hesitated. They were scared. But their fear was drowned in great expectations. "Let me ask the questions," said Jonnie. "And act as if you belong . . ."

The woman who opened the door to them was large and bosomy, friendly enough but puzzled by their presence. And making a sincere effort not to look at their stomachs. "Yes . . . can I help you?"

"I'm Joanna Olson? Who called about the house?"

The woman was obviously flustered. *"You're* Joanna Olson?"

". . . who called about the house for rent."

The woman looked past them, up and down the street, hopeful of seeing someone else. Her distressed eyes settled back on the three of them. "I'm so *sorry*, Mrs. Olson, but the house is already rented."

"How can it be rented? I just called!"

Maryanne's face flushed red. Ada was already backing away.

"I'm so sorry," said the woman, genuinely sorry.

"Thanks for nothing," said Jonnie.

"I am sorry," she said for the third time. She looked regretfully at the three of them. "Would you like to come in and have some milk and cookies?"

"I *knew* it!" wailed Maryanne. "They don't *want* people like us!"

They sat around the table of a sandwich shop reinforcing

themselves with malts. "Don't bad-mouth it," said Jonnie. "We just started."

"Let's go tomorrow," begged Maryanne.

"We haven't got time until tomorrow." But Jonnie's back ached, and Maryanne's head ached. They drank their malts and bolstered themselves with truth. Why when they had the money was it necessary to explain themselves? Why did they owe anybody an apology. Why was it a disease to be pregnant? Was sixteen a plague or something? Weren't they as good as anybody? Better probably?

Fortified with justice, they set out again. "If we don't find it this time," said Maryanne, "let's go to a show. Let's see the Hindenburg again, or the one where the boat turns over. I *need* something . . ."

The house was an old sloping frame, unpainted, ready to fall apart. The girl with the baby on her hip met them at the gate of the broken-down fence. "Sure you can rent it. We're leaving for Oregon to raise goats. Just move in and pay the rent under the name Smith. That's the name we got it under. Just send the money, no questions."

"How come you're moving?" asked Ada.

"Because I don't get along too well with termites and roaches. I'll take my chances with a heavy annual rainfall and goats. The heater doesn't work and the plumbing is clogged."

"Doesn't the landlord fix it?"

"The landlord is an envelope addressed once a month to Beverly Hills. Do you want it or not?"

"I think we're after something better," said Jonnie.

"Fat chance," said the girl. "If you have babies or dogs or if you're under fifty or more than one family to a house, forget it. It's termites or goats."

*

A House for Jonnie O.

They consoled themselves with Cokes and onion rings at Burger King. "I can't *stand* it anymore," said Maryanne. "Every time they say no, I die!"

"I'm getting a little depressed myself," said Ada. "Tell them who we are when you call them. Get the shock of it over first. Right this minute, I'd settle for a tepee in the land of my people."

"You can't have a television in a tepee," said Jonnie.

"You can put an aerial on a hogan. Call them first and let them know."

They started with a dozen dimes. By the fifth, Maryanne started to cry and had to go to the bathroom. Ada spit on the sixth for luck. Her braids were coming apart. Jonnie was so tired, she had to lean against the wall as she spoke. *Yes*, they were four. *Yes*, they were sixteen. *Yes*, most of them were pregnant. But they would take care of a house and pay first and last month rent and every other month rent — steady.

The man invited them to come on over.

Maryanne had washed the lipstick off her face, but she came back with swollen eyes. "I can't *stand* it . . ."

"Maybe — " Ada kept her voice casual — "maybe we got something." Jonnie shrugged, a small gesture. If you got too excited, it might be snatched away. Better to play it cool.

But the house was a nothing house, with uncut lawns and dirty windows. They sat in the car and looked.

"So what do you think?" asked Jonnie.

"I don't know . . ." said Ada.

Maryanne was entirely undone, not even good for an opinion.

"We can look at least," said Jonnie. At least if he said yes, it would break the bad-luck streak. It happened that way.

The man who ushered them in was fat-bellied and slovenly. He followed them with ferret eyes as they walked through the nothing rooms. Maryanne looked flushed and Ada was getting heavy-eyed. "You sign a statement for me that you're all over twenty-one," said the man.

Maryanne scratched her hand. "Didn't she *tell* you . . ."

"And that you're using the house strictly as a residence."

"What did you think we were using it for?" asked Jonnie.

"I want a deposit for breakage. I don't care what kind of parties you throw, as long as I'm paid for it. And if there's trouble, you're on your own."

"Dirty head in the pond," said Ada.

"I think I'm going to puke," said Jonnie.

"Do you want the house or not?" asked the man. "Take it or leave it."

"Shove it," said Jonnie.

They were shaken. They had to stop at the first short-order café for a sundae. Something rich. Something sweet. Something terrible as balm for the wound. They sat numbly around the booth, insulted, assaulted and hurt. "What did he think we *were?*" asked Maryanne. "I never fooled around in my *life!* Except for Arthur, I'm still a virgin!"

"The wild ones never got caught," said Ada. "They knew what to do. It's us who got it!"

"Sewers," said Jonnie bitterly. "They live in sewers."

The waitress hovered over them, waiting for them to order but listening in. They huddled closer together. "Now what?" asked Ada. "What do we do now?"

"Listen," said the waitress, "take some advice."

What Jonnie didn't need was advice from a waitress! "Butt out!" she said.

"No, listen," said the waitress. "I went through it myself. Only fourteen. Not even out of diapers myself."

Maryanne moved aside to make space for the waitress in the booth. "What happened? How did it come out?"

The waitress leaned into the circle. "Had to give it up. Only fourteen. My folks said they'd throw me out if I didn't."

"What was it?" asked Jonnie.

"Boy. Best thing to give it up. To somebody who's set up for it with a house. Somebody who can join the PTA."

"But don't you worry about him?" asked Jonnie. "And wonder. How he came out and all."

"Not much," said the waitress. "He's better off as it is, with somebody who can do something for him, not a fourteen-year-old kid wet behind the ears. So it's the best, you see. I don't think about him much any more. Only at night . . ."

They were too devastated to talk. They were headed home when they saw the "Houses for Rent" sign in front of the real estate office. "Here!" called Jonnie. "Stop here! Why are we dragging around and breaking our backs when we should have gone right to the real estate?"

"Why didn't we know that?" asked Maryanne.

"Because they were too busy teaching us poetry."

They were so weary that Jonnie had to shove the two of them through the door. But they were too close to stop now. That's when it might happen, when Fate turned her back, when Fate let her guard down. There were six desks in the office, five men and a woman. Everybody looked up when they entered. Five men looked quickly down, picked up phones and pencils and made themselves busy. The lone woman came forward, brought them to her desk and found them chairs. "Get a load off your feet."

"Let's get it straight," said Jonnie. "We want it straight. There are four of us. Three of us are pregnant. One of us has a baby already. We're all sixteen. We need a house. We have the money. We'll take care of the place. We don't give wild parties. We just want a plain, ordinary house to eat in and sleep in and take care of our babies."

"All on welfare?" asked the woman.

"What's wrong with welfare?" asked Ada. "It's steady."

"Anybody vouch for you? Any parent with good credit who would sign for you? Back you up?"

"We're emancipated minors," said Jonnie.

"Not in real estate. Without references and without credit, you're up a creek."

"But it's not fair!" said Jonnie. "What *is* it with them?"

"They want credit," said the woman, "and security. And young pregnant girls aren't secure."

"Don't we get any credit for being sixteen?" asked Ada. "Sixteen is as good as sixty!"

"You want it straight," said the woman, "and I'm giving it straight. You're pregnant, very young girls. A bad risk. Nobody is going to rent you a house, not anything decent. If you want to break up, I'll take your names and keep my eyes open for some small apartments. But you'll have to take what you can get. Your best bet is to find a friend with a friend who has a house for rent. You might as well understand that and make the best of it."

"It isn't fair," said Jonnie bitterly.

"Nothing is fair in real estate. Try the Salvation Army. Maybe *He's* fair, but, kids, the way the world is, don't expect fair. Life is ten percent down and don't make your payments late. If you're late, you're out. Don't expect more."

"Liar!" said Jonnie.

"I pray to God you're right," said the woman. "I wish I could give you more hope. Credit and security. The way it's always been, men get the credit, we hang on for security, and all we get are the babies. Things are changing, *maybe*, but not for sixteen-year-old pregnant girls on welfare. What else can I say . . ."

She sat in the tub, trying to understand it. She needed to think in a long, soaky bath. She dropped a yellow bath bead into the stream of running water. It was sucked under the confusion of turbulent bubbles, rose to the surface briefly, a yellow husk, and then nothing. Why? Why were they keeping it from her? Were they testing her? They meant her to have it, otherwise why had Billy come back? Why was it a hundred-to-one shot that she had found him when she called? Had she done something to provoke, to offend, to *defy*?

Her mother tapped on the bathroom door. "Jonnie! What's wrong?"

"Nothing is wrong. I'm just taking a bath."

"At half-past four in the after*noon?*"

She turned off the water and sank down, letting the hot creep up over her baby.

Her mother walked in. "You left the door unlocked." As if it had been an invitation. Now her mother closed the door and sat on the toilet seat watching her.

She sank deeper into the water. "Can't I have any privacy in here at least!"

"No. You're stuck in here and you'll have to listen for once. Abel has asked me to marry him."

She felt her baby turn in protest, hump up under her heart.

86

"You want to marry that nothing? Go ahead. You're old enough. You don't need my permission."

"Try to understand, Jonnie. It means a house. For both of us. I want us to stop fighting now. I want us to rest for a while."

"Rest as long as you like. Just leave me alone."

"He's a good man, a kind man. He'd be good for both of us. You're not too old to need a father."

"I *have* a father!"

"How many letters ago? Don't count on him. Let him go, Jonnie."

Even in here, they were on her! She couldn't even have any peace in *here!* "Marry anybody you want! But leave me out of it."

"Abel is returning to San Diego next week. He wants us both to come with him."

"Don't you understand what I'm *saying!* I don't want to *live* with you anymore!"

Her mother's face went blank, and then pale. "Don't make me choose. I can't leave you alone. You're still a baby yourself."

"I'm not alone! Billy is coming back!"

"The way he came back the last time? I know Billy Veller. I know all the Billy Vellers. This is my one chance, Jonnie. Don't make me lose my one chance."

"Go, then! You want to go! You're dying to go! Why don't you for once do what you want without putting it on me! For once, don't be a liar!"

"Then why can't you for *once* try to understand what I'm saying!" said her mother. "Why can't you for once talk to me, *talk* to me without *screaming!*"

Jonnie shut her eyes and sank deep into the soapy water.

"Who?" she asked softly. "Who's screaming?"

Her mother had no answer. The bathroom door closed, leaving her some silence at last.

Jonnie lay back in the warm water, breathing deeply to calm herself, and her baby. Then she saw it, the little mark, on the side of the mound of her stomach — the little stretch mark. She reached over for her dry skin cream and tried to rub it out. It wouldn't *rub* out. Like a little bird, trying to peck its way out of its egg. *"Please . . ."* she begged her baby. *". . .* wait! It's not *time* yet!"

6

A House for Jonnie O.

THE SKY was a pall of gray smog that hung like dank twilight over the city. Jonnie and Ada and Thalia slumped morosely on the back seat of the pregnant bus. A wheel hit a manhole cover, jostling its occupants. Voices rose in complaint.

"When . . ." asked Jonnie. "When did you find out?"

"Late last night," said Ada. "She finally got the nerve to ask her father if he would sign for credit, to get us the house, and he beat up on her."

"*Poor* Maryanne!" The pain to Maryanne hit her viscerally. She could have wept. "What did she *do?*"

"They called her sister in Sacramento again. Her sister is flying in. She said they'd meet us in Baskin-Robbins after school."

"They act like animals," said Thalia. "Worse. A dog wouldn't do like they do."

Jonnie lay her head against the window of the bus. "They . . ." she said.

*

89

Most of the class slept through a film called *The Terrible Twos*, which was about noisy children running around and banging pots. The nurse finally turned off the projector. "Nobody's watching. Why is nobody watching?"

Nobody knew why nobody was watching.

"But it's important that you understand this difficult stage, so you won't be surprised when it comes. So you'll be prepared."

"What I can't stand," said Alicia, "is bratty kids in markets who grab things and scream and make a fuss."

"Give 'em a good smack," said somebody.

"Don't you think," said the nurse, "that there might be a better way to train children than a good smack?"

"Like what?" asked Alicia.

"A loving parent is patient and firm, until the child learns to reason."

"You can't talk to no kid!" said somebody. "One good smack, he knows who's boss."

"Boss! Is that what you want to be to your children? A boss? Use your hands instead of your heads? Is that how you'd teach your babies?"

Not *babies*! they objected. Nobody would hit a *baby*! Not a *baby*! Was she crazy?

"But babies have a way of becoming children. That's what I'm trying to *say* to you! And hitting is an easy out. Hitting won't make happy children!"

"I just mean a smack," said Alicia. "Just to make him stop running around and be quiet."

"The two-year-old is not supposed to be quiet! He's supposed to run around and test his environment!"

"You can't keep chasing them all the time," said Alicia.

"But they take all your time when they're terrible twos.

90

That's why I showed you the film! You have to know that! Did you think they stayed sleeping sweet babies forever?"

"You fuss over them too much," said somebody, "they get spoiled."

"You can't spoil a baby with too much love," said the nurse. "Don't you listen to any of the films? Don't you ever hear what I tell you? If you love your child, you don't have to hit him! There are other ways."

"Just because she hits you," said Alicia sullenly, "that don't mean she don't love you."

"Who?" asked the nurse. "Who hits you?"

"*They* hit you," said somebody. "That's the way they do."

"*Where* do they hit you?" asked the nurse.

"They lock you in the closet sometimes," said somebody. "You get a little of that closet, you don't mind the belt."

"With a *belt?*" The nurse was getting upset.

"*Never* with a buckle." said Alicia.

"*Who* hit you with a belt!" The nurse was outraged.

"*Never* with no buckle!" Alicia turned away. "Anyhow, I deserved it."

"No you didn't!" said the nurse angrily. "No you didn't. Alicia, you *didn't* deserve it. You're silly, and you don't listen, and you do some dumb things, but, honey, you're as sweet as they come and you didn't deserve to be hit with a belt!"

Alicia laid her head on her arms. "How do you know how bad I was. Were you there?"

"The only reason I'm starting this unit on *Julius Caesar* . . ." began the teacher.

There was a *roar* of protest.

". . . is to show you that you have control over your own lives. 'The fault,' said Caesar, 'is not in our stars, but in ourselves, that we are underlings.' What did he mean when he said that?"

Nobody *knew* what he meant! Nobody *cared* what he meant!

"In Shakespeare's time, men still believed in signs and portents, that forces beyond our control and beyond our understanding determined what happened to us. When the heavens stormed, for instance, and lightning flashed, and meteors flew across the heavens, they believed it was a sign."

"I saw it in *The Haunting*," said somebody. "It rained blood."   .

"When Caesar went to the Senate, he had his augurers or fortunetellers kill a bird and pluck out its entrails."

"What has killing a chicken got to do with politics?" asked Alicia.

"What I'm trying to *say*," said the teacher, "is that signs mean nothing. Man makes his own fate if his eyes are open. But Caesar's eyes were closed with flattery and conceit. He had nothing to rely on but signs. And so his best friend stabbed him in the back."

"They do that," said somebody.

"Today we understand that the forces that determine our lives are not in our stars but in ourselves. And as women, we can be stronger than Shakespeare's tragic heroines who had to suffer and die for love. Like Portia, who had to stab herself in the thigh to prove to Brutus that she was worthy of his trust, and Ophelia, who drowned for Hamlet, and Juliet, who died for Romeo. And Cleopatra, who killed herself with an asp."

"Is that something sharp?" asked somebody.

"An asp is a snake."

"Shoo . . ." said somebody, "pills is easier."

"What I'm trying to *say* is that we don't have to destroy

ourselves for love. Love can be fruitful and joyful, if we understand it."

Jonnie raised her hand. The teacher seemed to be thankful that somebody had raised a hand at last! "What does it mean to knock wood?"

"In Shakespeare's time?"

"Now. In this time. What does it mean now? What kind of a sign is it?"

"No kind of a sign. It doesn't mean anything."

There was a general protest. Yes, it *did* mean something. And under ladders meant something. And black cats meant something.

"It was a pagan custom," said the teacher. "In olden times, like the times of our fairy tales, when pagan people believed spirits lived in trees, they would knock on wood to summon the wood spirits. It may have been the Druids, who believed that the oak and mistletoe were sacred. But today we know that there aren't any wood spirits in trees. Knocking on wood is an old superstition that doesn't really mean anything. What I'm trying to *say* is that the gods help those who help themselves, and why make a Shakespearean tragedy out of life when it's not necessary!"

"The thing with the leg," said somebody, "where she stabbed herself. I think I saw it."

"In *Julius Caesar?*" asked the teacher.

"In 'As the World Turns.' "

They waited for Maryanne and her sister in Baskin-Robbins, dosing themselves with double chocolate fudge with whipped cream and maraschino cherries and nuts, which might have serious side effects but which was the only thing

93

strong enough to support them in their misery, not only Maryanne's tragedy but their own private concerns.

"He lost his first appeal," said Ada, "but before the judge could find him guilty, his lawyer jumped up like Perry Mason and explained that he was the grandson of a great Oglala chief, and that the white man had stolen his land, and if he hadn't bent over, nothing would have fallen out of his pocket. When you take an Indian's land away from him, you can't put him in jail for just bending over, can you? So, they're holding him over until Friday."

Thalia licked chocolate off her spoon desperately. "My baby smiled today. A real smile. First time. But it was *her* he smiled at. He ain't even gonna know I'm his momma."

"It's not a smile," Jonnie consoled her. "He's too young to smile — it's gas."

"Don't tell *me* what's gas and what's a smile! I *know* what's gas and what's a smile! If we don't find a house, I'm gonna *kill* myself."

"I'm not using an asp," said Ada. "I'd rather hang myself."

"I'd rather drown myself," said Jonnie. "Just jump into the water and be done with it."

"I'll probably shoot myself," said Thalia, "but I'm so dumb, I'll probably miss."

Maryanne, poor wounded Maryanne, fluttered helplessly in the doorway, a hand covering an offended eye. Her sister, short like Maryanne, but stout and maternal, looked solicitously on, helping Maryanne over to a chair, sitting her gingerly into it. She pulled Maryanne's hand away from the eye. "Look at it! See what that animal did to my sister!"

The eye was purple, and swollen shut. The pale cheek was bluish with bruises. Maryanne tugged at her crucifix, almost apologetic. "It was an accident. He didn't mean it."

"An accident that he got boozed up? I don't understand this girl! Why aren't you spitting mad at him for what he did to you!"

"He said I didn't have any right to ask because I was a sinner. And I *did* sin."

Maryanne's sister hugged her. "Honey, you wouldn't know a sin if it looked you in the face. You're so innocent that you could walk through hell's fires and they wouldn't even scorch you. There's a difference between sin and a mistake. God knows it, if your own father doesn't. And if you haven't got the sense to know when that man is hurting you, I have to get you out of there."

"If we only had a house," Jonnie lamented, "we wouldn't need any of them."

The sister winced as she looked at the eye. "She'd be better off at St. Anne's. They'd take care of her at St. Anne's. A house isn't easy."

"She knows," said Maryanne. "She has six children."

"A house is no picnic," said the sister. "Don't kid yourself. It's hard taking care of a house."

"She's *my* sister *too*," said Jonnie, looking at the eye. "We're all sisters. We can take care of each other. We don't need to be taken care *of*. What *is* it about us that makes everybody look the other way? Or hit us like that just for asking to make a place for ourselves. It's a beautiful thing to have a baby — why do they make us so ashamed?"

"Are you all serious about this?" asked the sister. "I don't want to go out on a limb for you if this is only some sort of children's crusade."

"How old do you have to be," said Jonnie, "how many things do you have to have happen to you before they stop calling you children!"

95

"I can't leave Maryanne alone with that man," said the sister. "He'll kill her one of these days if he gets drunk enough. If you're serious, if you mean business, I have a friend who owns an old house out in Venice. It needs a lot of work."

"She's got us a house," said Maryanne, touching the edges of the swollen eye to test it. "I told you things happen for something. But I wish he had hit me someplace else."

She flew through the door, danced to the refrigerator, poured herself some milk and searched for what was to eat. She looked up when she realized that her mother was standing over the stove, stirring something, that the kitchen was a chaos of pots, that her mother, spoon in hand, had turned to watch her.

She felt so good, so happy, that nothing could rile her up. Not even Abel. "Abel coming for dinner?" she asked.

"Abel? No," said her mother. "It's for us. I came home early to fix lasagna. You know how long it is since I made lasagna? You used to love lasagna. I wish I had a chance to do more cooking."

"Lasagna gives me heartburn." She browsed through the refrigerator, found a doughnut and buttered it.

"Come and taste the sauce at least. This is wonderful sauce."

"Let Abel taste it." It was too late for lasagna. It was too late for everything.

"Why are you being so spiteful?" Her mother turned off the fire and went to the sink to run water for the washing up. "I'm trying to make it up to you. I came home an hour early."

"You didn't have to," said Jonnie. "I'm leaving. I found a house."

Her mother leaned over the steam of the sink, as if the wind had been knocked out of her, as if Jonnie had struck her. "Who? Who rented you a house?"

"Friend of Maryanne's sister. We're moving in on Friday. So you don't have to spend any more hours over a hot stove. Not for me, at least."

"You're leaving? Are you telling me you're leaving?"

"On Friday. So I hope everything goes okay for you and Abel. Goodby and good luck."

"Goodby?" her mother asked incredulously. "Goodby and good *luck?*"

"Once I'm out of your hair, you and Abel can live happily ever after. Admit it's what you want."

She couldn't sleep, thinking about her mother. She knew that in her mother's room it was the same. That's the way it had always been between them. Both of them cheated. Both wanting, both unsatisfied. Visions of mothers came to her. The mother in "The Waltons," the way she looked at you, her soft patience. She didn't do you such a big favor if she stood over a sink. Mothers like Shirley Jones or the reruns of "Father Knows Best" didn't fool her. She meant real mothers, from a thousand films she had seen. But she was cheated, all the way around. She was alien . . . a changeling. She and her mother spoke different languages. Different words with different meanings. And then they were both hurt when neither of them understood. If her mother tried soft words, they made her feel worse. And the hard words — she simply threw up a wall against them. Olivia de Havilland understood. And Joan Fontaine. And Bette Davis. She had a fantasy of the good fairy in *The Wizard of Oz*. But it didn't last. It was child's play. Her baby turned and reminded her. She

97

wanted to comfort herself with visions of herself as a mother, but all she got were bad feelings of herself as a child. She tried to conjure a fantasy of Billy, his eyes, his kind hands, his voice. But all she got was the sound of her father's voice. *Jonnie* . . . in a dark hushed whisper. *Jonnie* . . . She must have fallen asleep that way, curled up and holding her baby. She awoke cold, in the dark, to a shuffling sound in the hallway. A soft sound, like a mouse sniffling at the crack of the door. She looked out into the darkened hallway. A light clicked off in her mother's room. Then she saw them. The cardboard box of cups at her feet. She pulled them inside.

The blue china cups. Pieces of the broken cup had been carefully, painstakingly glued together.

She didn't want to look at them. She shoved them in the closet. "Too late," she said.

7

You Blocks, You Stones, You Worse than Senseless Things . . . O You Hard Hearts

SOMETHING WAS UP in the classroom. The tables had been shoved back and the chairs arranged in a circle. Donald Duck was already seated in the circle, waiting for them.

"What's he doin'?" asked somebody.

"Take a seat!" he called out. "I'm holding a seance."

They knew his corny humor, his trickery. They fell reluctantly into seats, feet out, not quite resigned, eyes closed, or upward in boredom, or whispering their morning's complaints to one another. Antoinette shoved in next to Jonnie and tugged at her sleeve. "The *house*," she wheezed.

"We're seeing it today," she said.

She tugged at Jonnie's sleeve again. "*Let* me . . . I *want* to . . ." She squinched up her face. "*Please* . . ."

Ada shook her head no. Maryanne shrugged. Thalia made a sympathetic face.

"*Please* . . ." wheezed Antoinette.

99

"She can come with us to see it at least," said Jonnie. "It's not fair for her to get left out of everything. At least she can come visit like a little sister."

"The purpose of this magical circle," said the counselor, "is to talk."

"About what?" asked somebody.

"Anything you want. Dealer's choice."

Silence fell over the circle. Somebody belched. Somebody scratched. Thalia took out her crocheting.

"Anything that comes to your mind. Anybody can start."

Somebody yawned. Somebody took off her shoe and scratched the bottom of her foot.

"*So,*" said Donald Duck, "since I get paid for it, why don't I start? How do you choose a man?"

"Who *chooses?*" said somebody. There was a smattering of laughter.

"Do I under*stand,*" asked Donald Duck incredulously, "that a bunch of good-looking sweet-natured girls like you, you don't do the choosing?"

That was the way of it. There was appreciative laughter, and some deep sighing.

"If you asked me, if *I* were a sweet young lady . . ."

"I would like to see *that!*" said somebody. "Shoo . . ."

"If I were a young lady, I would choose a man I had a lot in common with, who did things I enjoyed, who was kind and loving and considerate . . ."

"Shoo! He's so *funny!*"

". . . somebody who cared about how I felt . . ."

They found him amusing. They laughed at his good-natured nuttiness. "Old-fashion . . ." said somebody.

"That's old-fashioned? So what's new?"

"I want a *real* man," said somebody.

"A man who knows what he wants," said somebody.

"A man you can't push around," said somebody.

"I take that to mean," said the counselor, "that you can knock your heads against a stone wall and you can't get what *you* want, so you might as well give him what *he* wants, if you want to hang on to him."

That was about the way it was.

"And what is it he wants?"

"Shoo . . ." said somebody, "you know what a real man wants."

"And he doesn't want to take the responsibility for not making a baby, because he's a real man. Is that the way of it?"

"Real man don't shoot blanks," said somebody.

"Real man don't wear gloves."

"This is a classroom," said Alicia. "We're not supposed to be talking about the nasties."

"If sex is nasty," said the counselor, "if you have such a negative feeling about sex, how can you trust any man?"

Trust? They thought that was funny. "You can't trust no *man!*"

"But if you can't trust any man, how can you make any long-lasting relationships?"

Whoever heard of long-lasting relationships? Things didn't last. You get them while you can.

"But if you love somebody, if you really *love* somebody, don't you *hope* it will last and *expect* it will last?"

"Never say love," said somebody. "You say *love* to them, they know they got you for sure."

"But if you never say love," asked Donald Duck, "how do they know if you love them?"

"They know, you shove them around, you tease them, you

101

push them, you play around, they know, but you never say love because they get too sure and run around on you and then you have to get even and you run around on them."

"Are you serious?" asked the counselor. "Is *this* what's new?"

That was the way of the world. Watch "Search for Tomorrow." Watch "Edge of Night."

"What are they teaching you girls in history? The Revolution? The Civil War? You've got yourselves mixed up! You've got your love and your war mixed up! These aren't lovers you're choosing, these hard-rock he-men! These are combatants! These are opponents! Locking horns is love for *goats*, not *women!* You crazy girls!"

"*You* crazy!" they countered.

"So," said the counselor, "remember what I said."

"Shoo! What he said? He didn't say nuthin'!"

"Just don't forget the left eye of the donkey."

It wasn't until nutrition that it filtered down to the discussion level. They ate their sandwiches and their hidden Cokes and their bootlegged potato chips from brown paper bags and they talked about it.

"My boyfriend," explained Ada, "he's not like that. Nobody sees him the way I see him. Just because I got him off the streets. He looks like such a big shot. Like when he found this gun one time. He waves it around like he's in the Mafia, then when we're alone, when he's falling asleep, he rocks himself like a baby. He lays there and rocks himself."

"Take Arthur," said Maryanne. "Everybody bad-mouths Arthur. When we're alone, he *tries* to be nice, but just mention one word about his mother and he breaks out."

"Delonne Rashay One," said Thalia. "There was one real

102

bad rock. That time I was a fool for sure. He was so much sweet talk, then when he found out about my baby, he turned stone. I use' to think he was such a handsome face. But he turned real ugly. By that time he ask me to marry him. I didn't want to marry him no way. I didn't want to wake up every morning to that same ugly face."

"Then how come," asked Alicia, "how *come* you named your baby for him?"

Thalia tugged a loose string on her blouse. "Because I remembered the sweet. That baby is the sweet of him. And I can always look at my baby. A baby is never mean. They always love you."

"Army . . ." said Antoinette, brushing crumbs from her chin with her fingers.

"Army *what*, honey?" asked Thalia.

". . . my *boy*friend . . ." She squinched and blushed.

"Shoo, Antoinette, I never knew you *had* no boyfriend."

Antoinette grinned, buried her face in Jonnie's arm. ". . . took me to a show . . . bought me candy . . ."

"And then he ran out on you," said Ada. "Some rotten bum running out on a girl like you."

"He *didn't* . . ." wheezed Antoinette. "My momma won't *let* me . . ."

"Let you what?" asked Jonnie.

". . . *talk* to him . . . I *want* to . . ." Her mobile, flaccid mouth formed words, pleaded without sound, tried to make a statement. Antoinette wanted to say something. It begged to be said. She forced her thoughts into shape, made the statement a dozen times with her lips before the sound came out. "She . . ." she said, ". . . my *momma* . . . I *try* to . . . I'm slow . . . I *can* . . . she says *no*. . . she won't *wait* . . . I need to . . .*let* me . . ." The rest dissolved into nothing. Finally she gave up and rested her head against Jonnie's arm, and looked up with a plea. "You're my best teacher." she wheezed finally. "You teach me."

"Did you write to him?" asked Ada. "Did you tell him about the baby?"

Antoinette's eyes filled with tears.

"Leave her alone," said Jonnie. "She can't write."

"I *can* . . ." she wheezed, "in the *house* . . . like the other children . . ."

They fairly flew along the boulevard, except for those times when the Chevy developed its little cough, slowed down, chugged, spewed smoke as they urged it on to its wonderful destination. Ada hit the horn to warn other motorists out of her path. With a pace like that, she needed the whole lane to herself. Maryanne had to hold the bouncing, delighted Antoinette safe in the back seat. "We shouldn't have taken her!" she called. "Her mother will *kill* us!"

"She never goes anyplace!" called Jonnie. "She has a right to some fun once in a while. We'll drop her off on the way home."

They rolled through the streets of Venice, which was a shabby seaside town that had gone from riches to rags and was now tattered — but alive, and looking hopeful. Between the liquor stores and the Goodwill stores and the gas stations sprang pottery shops and plant shops and shops where seamstresses made bright gauzy blouses and patched blue jeans.

"We're here!" said Ada, swinging in toward the curb. As the motor shuddered, with its usual superfluity of energy, they saw it standing in a fine grove of eucalyptus trees, between a bakery and a milk dairy. A tall narrow house, it stood like an eccentric auntie, weathered, wind-beaten, peeling, a relic of better days, but erect, about half a block from the ocean. Upstairs, two dusty windows of a little tower room blinked at them, as if peering through glasses, and the sun's rays caught the blinking eyes.

"It's too good to be true," said Jonnie.

"It must be my grandmother's spirit," said Ada, "looking out for me. I love it."

Only Thalia was uneasy. "*Some*thin' will happen. I already love it so much, somethin' is bound to happen and break my heart."

"My sister paid us up for a month," said Maryanne, "so if the worst happens . . ."

"*What* worst?" asked Thalia apprehensively.

"*Any* worst, we've got a month at least. And she said there's some furniture in it, and to buy the rest secondhand."

Antoinette clapped her hands. "It laughed at me!"

"What laughed, honey?" asked Thalia.

"The house!"

The living room was old and large and high with beams and leaded windows. The sun filtered through the eucalyptus leaves and made shadow puppets on the walls. "You see!" laughed Antoinette.

Ada walked the bright center of the room. "You know those ghost pictures where the house has a cold spot? This house has a hot spot. Feel it."

"It's where the sun comes in," said Jonnie. But she knew better. She felt it too. The house was warm.

Antoinette, as if she had been there all her life, walked down the hallway, chose a door, opened it, solemnly went inside and closed the door behind her.

"It's a mistake," said Maryanne. "What if she gets used to it?"

"She can come and visit," said Jonnie. "A little sister can come over sometimes." Her own eyes were on the tower room. The tower called her. As if she had been in that house before, as if that room had always been waiting for her. As if she had seen it all before, as if she knew the story, as if it had happened and were happening again. She pulled herself up the steep narrow stairway. The room was at the top, a single door. It was her room.

It was almost a circle, with those two big windows that opened outward with a crank, a ledge outside and inside a window seat.

If her heart had been a bird, it would have taken flight and flown around that room. She could have exploded into a shower of stars. From her window seat she could see over the tops of buildings to the ocean. She could command the sea, like a voyager in a great crow's nest of a ship. Beautifully, joyfully alone, yet attached to the house in the same way her baby was attached to her, floating free, yet anchored.

She could hardly bear to sit there — it was too wonderful. She bent to her baby. "This is your house." Something more was needed, some ritual act to mark the occasion, something to signal the beginning of her new life. She leaned down and asked her baby: "Are you a boy or a girl?" She waited for the sign, one thump for boy and two for girl. Her baby stretched and turned. The thump was felt as a movement under her heart. Once. *Twice.* Her baby was a girl. She cranked open the windows, let in the bright expanse of ocean, spoke to the trees and to the green water and to the freewheeling gulls that squawked in from the sea. "I name my baby Lark . . . like a free bird." She closed the windows, looked

106

once more at the room to set it in her mind for that night's dreaming and closed the door behind her.

"They left the phone in!" called Maryanne. "All we have to do is connect it."

Thalia was measuring the living room with her hands. "You see that bad place? Where the picture was? I'm gonna paint butterflies. Okay with everybody?"

"More butterflies the better," said Ada. "This place sure needs a scrub-up. I want every corner of it clean. I want every piece of window to shine. I want to put flowers everyplace. I want to get us a kitchen table that's big so we can all sit around drinking coffee in the morning."

"If Arthur's mother comes around," said Maryanne, "can I have my wedding here? Can I wear white, do you think? If I put a little scrap of blue in it, would it be a sin?"

They would treat this house right. They would honor it and care for it. They made lists of things that needed attention. No small item was overlooked. The house had received them. It was in good hands. They started to leave for supplies.

"Antoinette," Jonnie remembered.

Antoinette curled over her notebook on the floor in the center of the room, her pencil poised over paper, the room a mess of discarded balled-up efforts. Her face was damp with perspiration, but her grin was victorious.

"Honey, we got to go now."

She hugged her notebook. *"No!"*

They had to pull her protesting from the floor. Jonnie squatted to pick up the notebook. There were words written on the open page. "She *wrote* something!"

Lovingly Antoinette accepted the notebook, stared, or

peered rather, at her words as if she herself could not believe the wonder of them. She smiled at the words, touched them with a finger to feel their substance. Embarrassed, but with pride, she offered the page to be read.

There were only three words, barely discernible in broad hills and valleys, the *t* uncrossed and the *i* undotted, but you knew in your heart what the words were:

drely belov it

"She's writing a letter to her F.O.B. telling him about her baby. She has a dearly beloved."

"I feel . . . " said Antoinette, "I feel . . . " The rest came in a sigh of contentment.

"This is a luck house," said Jonnie. "I named my baby here. She's a girl. Her name is Lark."

"Bird spirit," said Ada. "They'll like it in the land of my people."

They had to pull Antoinette out of the house.

Abel's car stood in front of the apartment. Okay. Let them make their plans. She had her own plans to make. She found him sitting alone at the kitchen table, drinking coffee. He caught her as she tried to pass. "Sit down. I want to talk to you."

"I don't want to talk to you. My mother's her own boss. She can do what she pleases."

"Is she?" asked Abel. "Is she her own boss? Who does the bossing in this house?"

"Is it any business of yours?" asked Jonnie.

"I love her," said Abel, "so it's my business. And you're part of her, so that makes you my business, whether you like it or not. Come on, Jonnie, tell me who's boss in this house? Who can fight a mouth like yours? Who can fight a sixteen-year-old pregnant kid? You think she's free to do what she

108

wants any more than you are? Neither of you are free yet to
go your separate ways."

"I've got my own place," said Jonnie. "So we're separate.
Good luck and have a good time."

"You're as separate as acrobats balanced on two ends of a
stick over the edge of a cliff. You should be helping each
other, but you both keep doing this act. She's as bad as you
are. Worse. She should know better than to play your game. I
don't understand it. Look what you could have done for each
other. It's such a waste." He stood up and left before she
could answer.

The accusation stung her. She called her court to session,
replayed the old injustices, reopened old wounds to the sympathetic eyes of her jury. But this time Abel stood up for the
prosecution, and left her shaken and unsure.

She went into the bedroom and took out her father's letters. Exhibit for the defense! She opened them and laid them
out and searched out lines she knew by heart. . . .*wish I could
be with you, Jonnie . . . bad luck . . . one of these days . . . couldn't
live with her, sweetheart. . . you could see that . . . if it could have
been different . . . if she would have been different . . . keep your eyes
on the clock.* If her mother had lived alone all these last years it
was her own fault. But Abel's mean words gnawed at her. It
wasn't *fair!*

Now she began to wonder why her mother hadn't been in
on the scene. Hiding out, probably, sending Abel in to do the
dirty work. The house was disturbingly silent. She walked
down the hallway and listened outside her mother's door. No
sound. She opened the door and looked in.

Her mother lay curled in rumpled blankets, her head buried in pillows. Two voices raged in her. *If only you could have
understood that some men have bad luck, if you could have been lov-*

ing and patient and sweet, I would still have my father. The woman lying on the bed was pitiful. *She's had hard times . . . give an inch . . . give . . .*

She was relieved when her mother stirred.

"Are you sick or what?"

"Nothing. Leave me alone."

She wanted just that. To leave this place now, to return to the place of her own. But Abel disturbed her. And now she wanted to break it cleanly, without rancor. "Want a cup of cocoa or something? Are you sick?"

"I don't want anything."

Old angers burbled up in spite of her. "I'm willing to make you cocoa. I'm *offering*. If you want to be a martyr, okay."

Her mother moved under the covers. "Tea."

She went into the kitchen and put the water on for tea. Yes. Better if it were done cleanly. Just be finished with it. The tone, the effort of the fight always left her limp. She was tired of it too. She just wanted it over. And she didn't want recriminations tagging after her like echoes.

She went into the bedroom closet for the box of blue cups.

The cup was beautiful, translucent when you held it up to light. She poured tea and sugared it. She made toast and buttered it and spread it with jam. She set the cup on the tray and brought it into her mother's room.

Her mother dragged herself up, looking terrible, red-eyed and pale. When she saw the cup, she began to cry.

Jonnie had *made* the offer, she had bent over backward, *double*, but she wasn't going to stand there and watch her mother cry!

Her mother reached over to the nightstand and laid a letter on the blankets. "It's from your father."

"For *me!*"

110

"For me. I wrote to him that you were leaving. He's coming to talk to you. He'll be here on Friday." Her mother didn't even look at her, just sat there warming her hands on the cup.

"How could you *write* to him if you didn't know where he was!"

"I knew," said her mother.

"All this *time?*" she asked in disbelief. "All this time you knew where he was, and you didn't *tell* me?"

"Yes."

"All this time you *lied* to me?"

"Yes," said her mother.

There was nothing more to say, or to be said. Life hung in a balance. The whirling forces of her Fate circled and observed, watched to see how she handled herself. It had all been said. What she had always suspected was true. Her father had *not* deserted her. Her father loved her. And her mother had kept her from that love. She had been cheated. But now it was coming right. She had a house. She had Billy. She had her baby. And now she was having her father again. While her mother, without anything, lay sick and punished. So wasn't that proof positive!

When the phone rang, she hadn't a shadow of a doubt but that it was Billy.

"*Bastards!*" he said, without even greeting her. "*Bastards! They make you promises, and they let you down.*"

He wasn't going to Alaska!

"*Sure you get a thou a week, but you know what it costs to live up there? By the time you pay all your expenses, you end up with peanuts. Try and believe anybody.*"

"We've got our house. When are you coming back?"

"*I don't know. I need a couple of days to get my head together.*"

She felt the tremor of fear. "You *promised.*"

She heard his disappointment. *"Don't you start on me. I said I just needed a couple of days to pull it together. I'll be back on Friday."*

The profusion of riches frightened her. She sat on her bed with her baby and tried to sort it out. Her father was coming back to her on Friday. She was moving into her house on Friday. Billy was coming back on Friday

Friday was a sign!

But of what?

Three Fridays! Three Fridays *had* to have a meaning. She reached over to knock wood.

Damn the counselor! Damn the teacher! She was too old and too smart to believe in fairy tales! There were no fairies! No wood spirits in her headboard! Then what was she knocking for? Who was she knocking for?

Her back was aching. Her stomach felt odd. She needed a sign, some confirmation, something, *any*thing to prove to her that Friday was a good omen. She reached for her *Movie Life*, closed her eyes and opened to a page, let her finger wander blindly, fixed on a passage, opened her eyes for the message:

Faye Dunaway's Mystery Miscarriage.

No! She could not accept that! If you didn't accept, you could get two out of three! Some believed it! *She* believed it! She opened to another page:

Liza Minnelli discloses how she shared Burt Reynolds.

No! Please, I'll do *anything. I'll stop biting my nails.*

She thought of the left eye of a donkey. *Who was she beg-*

ging? She opened the magazine for the third, for the last time, her final chance.

> Doris Day, in her most intimate beauty secret confides
> that one night of each week she coats her entire body in
> Vaseline.

It was as if the entire machine of her luck had gone haywire! As if the ties that connected her with her Fate had been torn out! If there were only Druids, if it were only a fairy tale, *then who was keeping her safe!*

Olivia de Havilland only looked down with that sad tender but half-questioning smile.

Mia's glance had a shrug in it.

Her old world was breaking up, and her new world was not yet ready! She pulled up her shirt, looked at her stomach, at the tightening swelling house that sheltered her baby. Other stretch marks crept up the side.

Please, there were only a few days more — a few dangerous days. *Help me!* She fell asleep holding her baby.

8

Wednesday's Child

"Why is Antoinette sitting at our table?"

Antoinette whimpered for them to hurry, holding her notebook close to her like some threatened treasure. Then she pointed to the office where her mother sat talking with the teacher.

"Why is your mother here?" Jonnie asked.

Antoinette pulled at her hair in distress, made little nasal frightened sounds.

"Jonnie!" called the teacher. "Can I see you, please."

The mother was a plain, ordinary woman, as unlike Antoinette as night to day. Small and dry, rather nondescript. But she smiled warmly at Jonnie. "I appreciate what you've done for Antoinette," she said with some feeling. "It's nice the way you girls have made friends with her. It's generous of you . . . and kind."

"It's okay," said Jonnie. "We like her."

"But this foolishness about a house — you have to understand that Antoinette is not like other children."

114

"She's not children," said Jonnie. "She's sixteen."

"In her body," said the mother, "but not in her head. She can't read or write."

"She can write," said Jonnie. "She's starting."

"Neither read nor write," said the mother firmly. "We've had her to specialists until we're past hope. And so we accept. And to encourage her after what experts have told us is impossible is an unkindness, and to encourage her to believe that life holds more for her than it does, Jonnie, is an unkindness. You may not understand that now, but you will when you're older."

Jonnie wanted to explain about Antoinette, but it was difficult to put into words. "She's our little sister. Can she just come and visit us once in a while, to help watch the babies?"

"I can't permit it," said the mother.

"Not all the time," said Jonnie, "But just once in a while, so that she has something to *hope* on."

The mother's smile was less attractive now and her voice had a tinge of iron in it. "It's out of the question."

"Just to give her *some*thing," said Jonnie. "Just a chance!"

"I gave her a chance once," said the mother darkly. "And you can see for yourself what happened. I'm not likely to be that careless again."

"She has a boyfriend. She wants to write to him. We're helping her write. We'll be her teacher."

"If that boy tries to come near her," said the mother, "I'll have him jailed."

"But she has nothing!" said Jonnie. "What has she got to dream about? We love Antoinette! She's like family. She's our little sister."

The mother's face turned cold. "She already has a family. We are her family. We've sacrificed our lives for her. We ask nothing in return. But I'm giving you fair warning, Jonnie. Either you stop filling her head with this nonsense, or I'll take her out of school."

"She's been locked in the toilet for a whole half-hour," said Alicia. "Better get the nurse to call an ambulance."

"She doesn't need an ambulance." Jonnie bent to see Antoinette's feet still firmly planted on the floor. She knocked on the door of the stall. "Come on out now."

"She might be killing herself," said Alicia.

"She's got nothing to kill herself *with*," said Jonnie. "You can't kill yourself with toilet paper."

"You can stuff it in your *mouth*," said Alicia. "Where there's a will, there's a way."

Jonnie knocked again. "Will you come out if *I* promise you? You can come and visit us once in a while, no matter what she says. We'll work it out. Do you believe me?"

The bolt of the toilet stall slid open. Antoinette stood holding her notebook and her pencil, her moon face tear-stained. "I *can* . . . " she whispered.

"Can *what?*" asked Alicia. "Kill yourself?"

"Can *write*," she said.

"I made up my mind," she told Donald Duck, "so don't give me any lectures."

"Give me some reasons, I won't give you lectures."

"My own place is a reason. I'll be busy. Anyhow, I'm not learning anything here."

"Sure you're not. But who knows. There's always a chance that you might accidentally leave the door open a crack. Stay around and warm a chair at least. Talk to the other girls. Keep up on current events."

"My father is coming," she said. "And my boyfriend is coming back. So who was right about luck? I know what I'm doing."

"I'm glad somebody does," he said. "Okay. So tell me. What are you planning for after?"

"After what?"

"After the baby is born."

"So you *admit* there's luck! *Admit* you were wrong! Did you know I had a feeling that my baby would be a girl? Go ahead. Tell me there's no such thing as a feeling."

"God forbid I should put down a mother's intuition."

"She's a girl. I named her Lark."

"Congratulations. From one bird to another. Greetings to Lark. I mean five years after, Jonnie. When Lark has nicely flown the crib for school, when she's busy trying her own wings, and you're still in the house stranded in your kitchen with waxy yellow build-up. Then what?"

Five years was too ridiculously faraway to consider. It was Friday that worried her. "What does Friday mean?" she asked.

"You'd rather play Twenty Questions? You're a hard case, Jonnie. Friday in what context?"

"Friday. Just Friday! What does Friday *mean?*"

"To me? Thank God it's Friday. I can sleep late on Saturday."

"Nothing else special?"

"What's special? Wednesday's child is full of woe, Thursday's child has far to go, Friday's child is loving and giving."

"Loving and giving. Then it's a good sign. Friday is a good sign."

"What sign? It's a poem."

"Today is Wednesday. What is *woe?*"

117

"Trouble."

"You see! We had trouble today with Antoinette. It *is* a sign! So things *do* mean something. And *luck* means something. You liars!"

"Hold it a minute," said the counselor. "That's a blow to the heart. You want to duel with me? You got a shot, I get a shot. I brought something to show you." He opened a deck of cards for her, spread them out on the desk. "Ever had your fortune told with Tarot cards? The ones with the pictures on them?"

"I thought you didn't believe in all that."

"Just listen. Did you ever take a good look at the death card?" He pulled it for her to see. "Look carefully at the way death sweeps the ground with his scythe. Look *carefully*. Where he cuts, new flowers begin to grow. He cleans away for new growth. So you tell me, is it a good sign or a bad sign? I told you, Jonnie, if you see clear, you can look into the mirror and get the answer. But if you're not ready to see something good, you look through a glass darkly. What do *you* want from Friday?"

"I want my house," she said. "I want my baby. I want Billy, and I want my father."

"So, a nice girl like you, why shouldn't you have the things you're ready for? The baby I can guarantee you. The house, if you're ready for it, because a woman gets a house, Jonnie, not a petulant kid. Are you woman enough for a house? Billy . . . who knows. Is he one of those rock-hard types? Your father . . . that I don't know. Does your father know how to love? We all fit together like a set of Chinese boxes. Tell me about *his* father."

"I don't understand you," she said.

"Don't let it throw you. You understand more than you

118

think you do. Let me tell you something about Jonnie O. I have great hopes for you. You're my candidate most likely to succeed."

"I hate that," she said. "I hate when counselors fill you full of bull — it's so phony."

"You and your animal symbols. I mean it, Jonnie. You have something rare in this classroom. You have immortal longings."

"Meaning what?"

"You bitch a lot. You flail around. You don't know for what yet, but you're looking for something."

"I know what I'm looking for. I'm getting it on Friday."

The teacher was definitely sulking. She had spent most of the morning in her little office reading while they had a vacation of crocheting, and since the crafts cupboard was open, they were also helping themselves to balls of yarn, *and* to felt, *and* to scissors, *and* as long as the math answer book was available . . . well, it was her responsibility, wasn't it? And if *she* wasn't being vigilant, well *shoo!*

But there wasn't any reason for her to sulk. When a teacher sulked, everybody felt guilty. Jonnie was leaving. The four of them were leaving. There was no need for the teacher to take it personally. So, as Jonnie was accidentally passing the little office, she just accidentally and casually dropped in.

The teacher sat reading from a small leather-bound volume of poetry and didn't even look up. This was beginning to make Jonnie sore actually, because this school, this pregnant school, should be a vacation from problems and anxieties, a place of respite, where you could talk and relax and think about babies. And teachers should be there to give assignments and mark credits, *not* provoke anxiety. She had nothing

119

against this teacher actually. It was just chance, and Fate, and the way things worked out.

"I just wanted to tell you," she said, "that I'm leaving on Friday."

"You're dropping out on Friday." The teacher spoke without looking up from her book. "Let's not play with euphemism."

So it was because of her — definitely. Pique in the voice — no mistaking it. "I don't know what that word means. But I'm leaving because I'm getting a house. You don't have to take it personal."

The teacher looked up, but kept a finger in the page. "Oh yes, it *is* personal. I tried to teach four girls and I failed. So that most assuredly makes it personal."

Jonnie shrugged. Her own damn fault! "I warned you about the poetry."

The teacher turned to Jonnie with smoldering eyes. "*And* the history, *and* the math, *and* the paragraphing, *and* . . . *and* . . ."

"Oh *that*," said Jonnie.

The teacher turned back to her book, as if she were looking for answers she couldn't find. "You all march to the tune of a different drummer, and I don't know how to play your tune."

"I *never* know what you're talking about," said Jonnie. "I just wanted you to know that it's nothing you did wrong."

The teacher wasn't buying it.

"So what's Friday?"

"Look at the calendar," said the teacher. "You don't need me for that."

"No. I mean what *is* Friday. Like with your poetry, and symbols. Like Shakespeare. What does Friday *mean?*"

The teacher turned to Jonnie curiously, with surprise, and

then her glance softened. "Are you giving me a gift? A goodby present? Are you asking me a question at last?"

"I just wondered what Friday meant."

"Friday? The word comes from Freitag, Frigga's day. Is that what you want?"

"Who's Frigga?"

"Frigga is the wife of Odin. An old Norse god. Frigga is the goddess who knows the future."

"Does she tell it! What does she tell!"

"She doesn't. She tells it to no one. Sometimes Frigga is confused with Freyja. But both of them are goddesses of childbearing. Sometimes they fly in the form of birds. They're called the weeping goddesses. Frigga is the wife and the mother. Freyja is the mistress. But they both weep."

"Then is it a lucky day? If it's fertility, then it's lucky, isn't it?"

"Jesus was crucified on a Friday."

"Then it's *un*lucky," she said in alarm.

"Friday is a holy day. It's the beginning of the Jewish Sabbath."

She was relieved. "Then it's lucky then . . ."

"Hangmen hang on Friday. Witches confess on Friday."

The frustration overwhelmed her. "What good does it do you to *know* anything! What good is it when it doesn't give you the answers!"

"Listen to me, Jonnie!" The teacher was also frustrated. "I haven't got the kind of answers you need. And I can't promise you anything it's not in my power to give. Do you understand me? I'm a *teacher*, not an alchemist! I can't change the base metal of anyone's life with Government or Typing One or Math. Do you know why I want you to read poetry? To *read poetry* and *feel* poetry? Because poets have answers that I don't

121

have. They come closest to the heart. Do you know what I'm saying? In the hieroglyphics of poetry, you'll find answers. I'm only a teacher, Jonnie. I know what you need, but all I have to *give* you is poetry."

"This is some crazy house!" Ada, heavy-bellied, her braids tied around her head, smiled up from where she bent on her knees, scrubbing the dirt-encrusted kitchen floor. "They've been ringing the bell all afternoon. Two girls down the street with babies want to be friends. Venice has a Free Clinic and a Family Planning, and we're supposed to join Venice for the Venice Poor and not let the landlords push us around, and if an old lady comes around and calls us degenerates, we're supposed to ignore her because she's the local crazy."

Jonnie had been stirring paint for Thalia, who was painting butterflies in the living room. "I looked to see what the church was down the street," she called to Maryanne, who was sweeping the porch dust into a dustpan that Antoinette held for her. "It's called St. Jives. Is that a new saint or something?"

"I *hope* he's a new one," said Maryanne. "I can *use* a new one for a change. The old ones won't let me use anything but rhythm, and I can't catch *on* to rhythm. If Arthur and I get married, would it be a sin to use foam, do you think? I mean, if I can get it in a drugstore without a prescription, do you think it's a sin?"

Thalia, paint-spattered and radiant, her hair a bouquet of color, called in from the living room. "Come and see! It's so beautiful, I even surprise myself."

The wall was an astonishment of butterflies. They started in one corner, near the floor, as a nest of eggs. The eggs hatched into small green butterflies that fluttered and grew and took color and spread like a cloud and spilled across the wall in wild jeweled splendor, up toward the ceiling and around the corner of the stairwell toward Jonnie's room, floating skyward.

"I never saw a thing *like* it!" said Ada.

"There won't be another house in the world like it!" said Jonnie.

Antoinette walked toward the wall and reached out to touch.

"It's still wet, honey," said Thalia. "It's a shame she can't stay, she loves it so much."

Maryanne was looking at the eggs. "Aren't butterflies supposed to hatch out of *cocoons* or something?"

Thalia considered. She let the information simmer in, fall into the slots already established in her bank of information, but came to the deeper understanding. She stood close to the wall. The butterflies seemed to flutter around her. "Cocoon butterflies come from *science*. These come from a different place!"

They all understood.

Antoinette, mesmerized by the butterflies, squinched suddenly, a little soft sound, like a sheep bleating.

"What's wrong, honey?" asked Thalia. "What's the matter?"

"She's been doing that for an hour," said Maryanne. "I think she doesn't feel so good, after all that with her mother. It always gives me a bellyache to fight with my mother."

"Where does it hurt you?" asked Ada.

She was afraid to tell, clung to Jonnie's arm, buried her face, but squinched again.

"Do you have a pain or something?" asked Jonnie.

Antoinette shook her head into Jonnie's arm.

123

"Just tell where."

". . . my back," she whispered.

"Same thing with me," said Thalia. "It's her time. For sure."

"*Can't* be. She's in her seventh!" So they sat around and petted her like an ailing baby sister. She squinched again, but this time she moaned. She couldn't hide the pain.

"We better get this girl home!" said Thalia. "Sometimes when it comes, it comes!"

Antoinette held on to Jonnie and pleaded, "*No!*"

"I think we better take her to the hospital," said Ada. "Somebody call her mother."

Antoinette looked helplessly from one to the other, begging for something.

Jonnie hugged her and rocked her. "The hospital . . . now."

"No!" she screamed. "I don't *want* to! They'll *hurt* me!"

They had to explain it to her with patience, like a little sister. "It's time to have your baby now. It's time for your baby to be with you. You'll see it."

"I *told* you we shouldn't have brought her," said Maryanne.

"She had a taste of it at least," said Jonnie. "Something is better than nothing." They led Antoinette sobbing silently to the car. Ada started the motor. Maryanne sat in front to help warn traffic out of the way. Jonnie and Thalia held Antoinette safe against them in the back seat. She looked up at them, wet-eyed. "Will she let me buy things for my baby?" she asked, "like the other children . . ."

The little Chevy moved smartly through traffic. Antoinette was lying down now, watching their faces as they petted her.

The car coughed, spurted smoke, hesitated. "Don't!" Ada thumped the dashboard. "Not *now!*" She jammed her foot down on the accelerator. The car leaped forward, swerved around a couple of cars, flew like an arrow.

The sound of a siren floated behind them. "Just what I need!" called Ada.

"She'll have a police escort, like on TV!" said Maryanne. "They escort you if it's a baby."

Ada pulled over to the side of the road and waited for the policeman. "You're going to hate me . . ."

"Since *when*," moaned Jonnie, "since *when* don't you have a license!"

"Can we lift the little girl into the police car?" asked the officer.

"No!" wailed Antoinette. "I *won't!*"

The officer wasn't happy about driving the Chevy. He verbalized his complaints. "Don't bad-mouth it," Ada advised him. "It's not very happy about you either."

Antoinette's mother waited for them at the emergency entrance like a Fury, trying to take Antoinette out of their hands. Antoinette screamed and refused to be lifted into the wheelchair. She hugged them all and begged them not to leave her.

Antoinette's mother shoved them rudely back. "You see what you've done — you and your house."

Maryanne slipped a set of rosary beads into Antoinette's hands. "Ask the Virgin," she whispered. "She'll make it easy for people like you."

They tried to follow her into the emergency entrance, but the mother would not permit it.

"Shoo . . ." said Thalia helplessly.

She spoke for all of them.

*

125

"Don't *any* of you girls have a license?" asked the officer.

Ada pointed to Thalia. "She has it. She was supposed to be driving, but she had to sit in the back with a sick friend. So don't try to push me around. I'm an American Indian and I got rights."

Thalia hopped nervously, as if she needed to go to the bathroom. " . . . parallel park!" she said.

"Parallel park *what?*"

"Didn't . . ."

"Then can I call somebody's mother to pick you girls up?"

Thalia's mother stormed into the hospital parking lot, barrelled out of the car like a marine, took off with both hands after Thalia. Thalia, whimpering, eluded her. "I thought you was dead!" screamed her mother, making a vain pass at her. "When the police called me, I thought you was *dead!* When are you gonna let me have some *peace,* girl!"

"I tried to explain to them, ma'am," said the officer. "They have to have a license to drive a car."

"They don't give no license to no fool!"

They reached the haven of Baskin-Robbins too exhausted to eat. They spread their list of necessities out on the table. "Phone gets turned on tomorrow," said Ada. "We have to pay a deposit on the gas. Somebody buy light bulbs so we have light. And if the Salvation Army delivers the stuff, I guess we can move in on Friday like we planned."

They waited for the blow to descend, or the earthquake to strike, or the fire, or the volcanic eruption. They waited for Fate to make her move. There were no objections, no signs, or counterindications.

"So I guess we move in!" said Jonnie.

126

"Double pistachio!" called Maryanne.

"Hot fudge on vanilla with nuts!"

"Double chocolate with marshmallow!"

Maryanne's joy was short-lived. Her face went pale, then flushed into their two spots of fire. "Hail Mary. It's *his mother!*"

Arthur Hammerman tried to signal Maryanne about something. The woman who pushed behind him shoved him away and walked over to where they were sitting.

Arthur's face was aglow with a new outbreak of acne. "Where have you *been?*" he asked Maryanne nervously. "My mother said she would *meet* you." He looked tentatively toward his mother to check how she was behaving. "She might take us out to dinner, and we'll talk about it."

Mrs. Hammerman looked scornfully at the four of them. "Are you sure you picked the best of the litter?"

"Please . . ." Arthur begged. "You *promised!*"

She looked Maryanne over like merchandise, her face, her stomach. She frowned. "It's a good thing your father is dead. Bring her outside. Let's take a look at her."

"Fix yourself up!" said Arthur frantically as his mother walked out. "Do something with your hair! I can't believe she's coming around."

"You don't honestly think she's going?" said Jonnie. "Do you honestly think she's going after what your mother said!"

"I am." Maryanne dumped out her purse looking for her comb. "She wants to meet me."

"But she insulted you!" said Jonnie. "Don't you know that you've been insulted!"

Maryanne pulled the comb through her hair and began to paint on some lashes. "She wouldn't have *asked* me if she didn't want to. She means well."

*

127

It was late that evening when he called.

"Been lying here thinking about us, honey."

"Where are you!"

"Up in Mendocino."

"Why are you in Mendicino? We're ready to move in on Friday! You could be camping out here!"

"Been straightening out my head about our baby."

Her breath caught. Her chest was tight. "Are you all straight now?"

The pause was a long one, an interminably long one. *"All straight, honey."*

She left it at that. That was enough, all she could handle for now. She gave him the address.

"I love you, Jonnie," he said. Before she could think of a response, she heard the click of the phone.

He loved her.

He had said he loved her. Himself he had said it. It seemed to her that she had waited her whole life for someone to say "I love you" of his own volition. It had come full circle, from that first call. The needle of the compass spun, its full circle. Billy Veller loved her, and he was coming home.

Only one thing puzzled her.

He had said *their* baby.

Why was it she wanted to think of Lark as *her* baby?

9

Thursday's Child

THE HOUSE could have been there forever, dormant, but now awakened to life. The old furniture brought by the Salvation Army truck, shoved into place in the spruced and polished butterfly's nest of a room, could have been left as a legacy from a grandmother, as familiar as if she had known it forever. As if the house were a part of memory, mellowed by time, and as much a part of her as any place she had ever really lived, *more* a part, because she loved it. Ada's floors were jewels, scoured and waxed and polished. Jonnie cleaned windows, washed away the dust and let in the bright day. Maryanne tried to figure out how to put the little metal rollers of the window shades into the slots. All occupied, so that nobody was ready for the slamming of the front door.

"*Thalia!*"

Thalia had slammed the door and leaned against it, her face contorted.

Something terrible had happened to Thalia!

Her hair had been chopped off, in awful spiky clumps.

"Who *did* that to you," cried Ada. "We'll *kill* him."

The door was shoved open behind her. She leaned her weight against it to try to hold it closed, but her mother pushed her way in, winced as she looked at the terrible hair, dried her own eyes on an already damp handkerchief. "You see what this fool done to herself? You see how she made her pretty self ugly."

"*I cut it off!*" screamed Thalia. "I cut it off because I'm too ugly to have hair!"

"Tell them," said her mother, drying her eyes. "Tell them what kind of fool cuts her own hair to hurt her own self." Thalia's mother looked half in pity, half in defeat at her daughter. "Only a fool hurts herself to make things better. Let her go look in the mirror and thank the Lord she still has a momma who loves her, even with that head of hair."

"*I hate you.*" screamed Thalia.

Her mother dabbed at wet eyes. "No she don't. We're goin' back to her grandma in Louisiana. We're puttin' her back in school where a teacher don't let you get away with murder, where she can learn her place, where they stand over her and let the backs of her knuckles know when she's doin' wrong, where they won't let her slide."

"They're taking my baby back to Louisiana," wept Thalia.

"So say goodby to your little friends," said her mother, "and thank the Lord that time cures all fools."

They hugged her and petted her and kissed her, not only to comfort her but for themselves. They made her hot cocoa and brought out doughnuts for themselves and for her, buttered them and ate them and wept. Maryanne tenderly fingered the shorn hair. "Oh, how *could* you . . ."

"First I was gonna kill myself. They let me get so close this time before they snatched it away . . . and then I knew if I died they would have my baby. I wasn't gonna let them have him. So I just cut my hair off."

"Stay with us," said Jonnie. "Stay here and get yourself a job and when you've got enough money, go back there and take your baby and bring him back here where he belongs."

"Can't leave my baby," she said. "Can't!"

It was a while before they all remembered the house.

"There's no house without my baby," said Thalia, begging them to understand. "The baby *is* the house. When I cut my hair off, I got smart about somethin'. I learned somethin'. I ain't no fool no more. I'm shuttin' up and goin' with and hatin' them and waitin' my time. One of these days I'll be my own boss. And when I'm my own boss, I'm takin' my baby and I'm comin' back. I know he's my baby and he's gonna know he's my baby, no matter what I got to do to make him. I suffered . . ." Her voice had suffering in it now. "And I ain't nobody's fool no more."

The horn sounded outside, like doom.

"You mark my words," she vowed, "you wait and see as sure as I'm alive, I'll walk in here one of these days with my baby, and everybody will say, 'Who is that beautiful baby? Who is the momma of that sweet child?' Her eyes settled on the butterfly wall, on the wild bright rush of butterflies. She held a hand over her mouth. Her tears came fresh. "Martin Luther King is dead," she wept.

They sat for a long while over cold cocoa, all thinking the same question. "Can we swing it without her?" asked Jonnie finally.

"If we eat hamburger," said Ada.

"Are you crazy?" asked Maryanne. "Do you know what hamburger costs these days?"

131

"Are we moving in tomorrow or not?" It was unthinkable that it should be *not*, because this was *her* house as much as Lark was *her* baby!

"My sister paid us up for a month, at least."

"Can we get someone else?" asked Jonnie. But that seemed unthinkable because this was their *family* house. And when she remembered that, the answer was obvious. "Antoinette!"

"But Antoinette's a retard!"

"No she's not. They just keep her slow, is all. You saw how she was starting to write with us? All the doctors said she couldn't write, but she was writing."

"But we'll have to take care of her! What if we move away or something. Who would take care of her?"

That anybody should want to move away from this house seemed unthinkable. "She's alone," said Jonnie. "Nobody else loves her. What if she really were our little sister? A home is a place where, when you have to go there, they have to take you in."

"I think Robert Frost said that," said Maryanne.

"Who?" asked Jonnie.

For Antoinette, for the little sister who had a baby, they bought a giant panda with glass eyes. Not for her baby, for *her*. Them*selves*, they would have loved that panda. They all squeezed into the hospital elevator holding it. They all hated hospitals and the panda made it more tolerable. "Doesn't look much like 'Medical Center,' " said Ada. "How come the orderlies have such rumpled jackets?"

"Let's try to talk to her without her mother," said Jonnie. "Let her decide something for once by herself."

Antoinette's mother would have turned them away, but Antoinette called out to see them, her eyes bright with the

132

panda. She smiled at them wanly from the bed, held her hands out for the doll. But her mother took it from Maryanne and put it on the dresser. "I'll keep it safe, with the other things for our baby."

Antoinette watched her mother and the panda. Her eyes were not slow. Her eyes saw everything.

"God help her," said the mother pityingly and with a martyr's pain. "She didn't even know what was happening to her. But mother was there, and now she'll come home with mother and help take care of our baby."

Antoinette looked at her mother dully, and back to them. She squinched her face, and then turned away. "She isn't *going* to . . ."

"Going to *what*, honey?" asked Maryanne.

But Antoinette wouldn't say anything else. She turned away. As if all the electricity had gone out of her.

Jonnie cleaned out the last of her old room. She stacked the movie magazines and took down the glossy pictures, friends from all the late-lates of her life. She loved Joan Fontaine, of the crooked sweet smile. But Joan Fontaine was an old lady now, with an aging face. And someone had said that Elizabeth Taylor was sick with something. Or she had read it somewhere. Cher was having trouble herself, still married to the wrong man. So that all the rich costumes and all the loyal fans didn't keep her from having hard times, just like everybody else.

None of it seemed real.

Only the house was real. And her baby.

This was the end of her obsolete life.

Lark stretched, reminding her.

She tried not to think of it most of the night, and only slept toward morning.

10

Always Go for the Eyes

So THIS WAS their last breakfast together. Her mother had set a fancy table, more food than either of them could eat. Jonnie wasn't hungry. And her mother, who poured coffee into the blue china cups, had fixed her attention on the cup itself. She fingered the cup and when it was empty, she held it up to the light, looking for something in the translucent china. "I wonder," she said, "I wonder what I was saving it *for?*"

"Ada's picking me up in the car. My suitcase and the other boxes are out on the porch."

Her mother nodded. "I'm driving down to San Diego with Abel. I don't want to be here when your father comes. I'll phone when I come back."

"You don't have to do that." There was no angry intent to the statement. It was plain fact.

Her mother seemed not to have heard her. "There are bound to be things you need."

"I have everything," she said.

134

"We're sending your bed over to the house. So it won't feel so strange."

She nodded her thanks.

". . . but you'll phone me before the baby comes. You'll call me when it's time."

"Won't be necessary," said Jonnie. "My friends will help me." Jonnie rose to leave.

"Please . . ." her mother began.

She couldn't stand to wait for the rest of it. "Goodby now," she said. "Have a nice wedding."

Odd how you got used to a place, even a nothing place. Even a classroom with its boring history and its stupid poetry and its crazy counselor. You just got *used* to it. The nurse was putting on the reel of film for the morning movie. The teacher sat in the office registering two new girls, a Chicano girl with a low hairline and a hard-set mouth and a black girl, very shabby, who seemed to be refusing to put her lunch into the kitchen. The nurse dimmed the lights for the film. Even the scratchy sound of the old projector was an old familiar joke.

"Let's come back sometime," whispered Maryanne. "To visit."

"Just for old times," said Ada.

The scene that materialized on the screen was an empty street at night. The title flashed across the image: *Self-Protection for Women.* A woman walked down the street, the sound of her heels echoing hollowly on the pavement, a well-dressed woman, a purse slung over her shoulder. A man began to walk behind her, slowly at first, and then quickening his steps. The whole class sat up alert. Now he ran toward her. She turned and saw him. He tried to grab her.

"*Watch it!*" called somebody.

She threw up her elbows to make space between them, came down hard on his instep with her heel, brought her knee sharply up into his groin. He screamed in pain. She raked his face with her fingernails.

The voice of the commentator rose over the cries of the attacker, who was fighting off a barrage of hair spray. "Always go for the eyes."

The class was shouting encouragement. *"Get* him! *Kill* him! Fix him *good!"*

The teacher came running out of the office. "Turn that *off!"*

The nurse switched off the projector. The sound ground down as their shouts of protest rose. "Let us *see* it! We *want* it! We *need* it!" Already their notebooks were open, their pencils poised.

The nurse turned on the light. "I misread the title. I thought it was contraception. But look at them, will you! They're taking notes! All my films on the terrible twos and psychology and creative playthings and vitamin deficiencies and for *this* they're taking notes?"

"It's *boss!"* they shouted. "It's *good!* First good film we ever *had* in here and she makes us turn it off! Shoo . . ."

The teacher held her ground, righteously indignant. She raised her hand for silence, like the Statue of Liberty. "I will not have my classroom used for survival training. It's *life* I'm preparing you for, not combat!"

But this *was* life! This was the way it *was!* You had to *protect* yourself! Or they *got* you! They got you one way or the *other!* They got you sooner or *later!*

She searched their faces for an answer. "Is *this* the kind of world you want for your babies?"

What other world *was* there!

"The world you create for yourselves," she pleaded. "The

world you create for your children. Each one *teach* one." She
opened her book of poems.

"No!" they roared. Not *this* time!

The poem was called *Renascence*.

They didn't want a poem by any name! Anyhow, if they
couldn't understand the title even, how could they understand the poem!

"It comes from the French word 'naître to be born! That's
what our class is all about, isn't it? Being born?"

This was an English class! They were supposed to be study-
ing English!

She read her poem above the clamor of rebellion. They
didn't *want* poetry! They needed raked eyes, damaged groins,
blood!

" 'The world . . .' " she read.

No! They wanted to know how to use the *heels!*

> "The world stands out on either side
> No wider than the heart is wide . . ."

No! They wanted the *nail file! A comb* to the eyes! *Hair* spray!
Cut him! *Blind* him! *Knee* to the privates!

> "Above the world is stretched the sky, —
> No higher than the soul is high . . ."

You need a *gun* by the side of the bed, and a *knife,* and a
stick.

> "And he whose soul is flat — the sky
> Will cave in on him by and by."

"I'm not saying," she begged, "that the world on the film
does not exist, but do you have to admit to it? Fight it! Do not

go gentle into that dark night! Don't learn the rules of the game! Don't re-create it for another generation! Make the world as high as your soul is high! Let your babies know that this high world exists, at least."

She was crazy! More crazy poetry! How can the world cave in and the sky fall down? Except in a Japanese movie? How can you have a flat soul? The soul doesn't *have* a shape!

"Renascence means rebirth! To be born again!"

Only Jesus can be born again! And you're not supposed to be talking about Jesus in school!

"You can be born again. The poets promise it! The sun also rises, and the phoenix rises from the fire."

There *was* no other world! It was a *lie* to say there was! People *said* there was, but there wasn't! That's the way people *were!* Who *wouldn't* want it to be different!

The mood of defeat overrode the teacher's poem. Poems were supposed to make you happy, weren't they? Well, they weren't happy. In fact, everybody was depressed, even the teacher.

And so they were all relieved when the door shoved open and the counselor walked in carrying a wrapped package. "I heard all the yelling. Am I too late for the surprise party?"

"What surprise party?" asked Maryanne, her face already flushing into red spots of excitement.

It was a house shower! For *their* house!

Crepe paper appeared, and cups and napkins, and bowls of red fruit punch, and two kinds of Dolly Madison cake, and Twinkies, and chocolate chip cookies. And wrapped gifts! Maryanne was already in tears. "I can't *stand* it!" They were embarrassed and pleased, and touched. They let their house get congratulated and their departure lamented.

*

"Open my box first," said Donald Duck. "I like to make the biggest splash. Get it?" he added. "Donald *Duck* . . . the biggest *splash?*"

They moaned over his pun, lovingly. He was a funny duck.

Jonnie pulled the paper off the package.

A toaster oven! How boss! How fine! How *expen*sive!

"To warm up your mushy white bread," said the counselor. "So why don't you keep a nice house and go to school also? We'll miss you. See what nice folks we are?"

"We have too much to do," said Ada.

"Okay. After you get tired of cleaning the toilet bowl ring and shining your plates until you can see your face in them. Then what?"

It was too far away to consider.

They opened the rest of their gifts.

They waited until Alicia came into the bathroom. "Thanks for the super gift," said Jonnie.

"I left on the price tag," said Alicia. "In case you get too many plastic glasses. Just take it back to Newberry's."

"Listen," said Ada offhandedly. "The house is really great. You have to come see it."

Her eyes were dying to come see it.

"Hey — now that Thalia can't come in with us, how about you?"

"Boy," she said, "boy. Thanks anyhow, but I'm getting married. My boyfriend finally came around. His grandma got *to* him and told him that if he didn't marry me he would burn in hell. So he came around finally."

"So you'll need a house then."

"He's going into the navy. He can't stand babies. But I told

139

him, if you can't stand babies, you better stop standing the nasties."

"So you'll need a place to stay then. Come stay with us. How about it?"

She wanted to. You could see in her eyes she wanted to.

"It's like *this*," she explained. "My mother has these spells and all? So she has to have somebody watch her. I mean, if it's your fault from when you were born and all, then you have to stay, don't you? Boy, who wouldn't want their own place." She hovered between desire and indecision. They knew she wanted to. "I'll tell you what," she said finally.

"What?"

"I'll write *Dearabby*."

She wanted to say goodby to the teacher. Not that they had been friends or anything, but in her own crazy way, the teacher was tenacious. You had to hand her that.

The teacher was reading her *Renascence* from the little soft leather-bound volume. "Look," said Jonnie, searching for the right words, "I'm sorry if I hassled you."

The teacher closed her book. "You haven't hassled me. You've puzzled me."

"I just want to say you did your best and everything. I understand what you said. I'm just dumb about poems."

The teacher handed her the leather-bound volume. She looked at it, felt the soft leather and handed it back. But the teacher wouldn't take it. "It's yours now."

"Why is it mine?"

"An old superstition. Once you accept a leather-bound copy of Edna St. Vincent Millay from an English teacher, you have to keep it and pass it on."

It was a kindly lie. She tried to return it.

"It's an old superstition. If you try to give it back, the sky will rain fire."

"Give it to someone else. I don't understand poetry."

"Then just touch the cover. If you don't understand with your ears, you might with your fingers."

"You're crazy, you know it? You're as crazy as Donald Duck."

"Thus spake Zarathustra," said the teacher.

"I never understand a word you're saying."

"Sometimes I don't understand it myself," said the teacher. "It's divine inspiration."

She opened the book and scanned some of the lines to find even one line she might admit to liking, for the gift's sake. "April comes like an idiot, babbling and strewing flowers," she read. "I wish I could figure it out. But I can't. Why is a season an idiot? How can April babble? I don't know what *strew* means."

"That's one line," said the teacher, "I hope you never have to understand."

As odd a duck as the counselor. A soft person, actually, with tired eyes. "Why do you stick around here?" asked Jonnie. "Why don't you teach kids who go in for this kind of stuff?"

"I told you. You're a six-month embryo. How do you know yet what kind of stuff you'll like? And . . ." she said.

"And?"

"And once in a while I meet someone like you, Jonnie, someone who doesn't just give up and go blank behind the eyes. Someone who's fighting in a way she doesn't understand. And it warns *me* not to go blank behind the eyes. So, maybe I'm waiting to see what happens in the next chapter."

*

141

The counselor hugged them at the door, big bear back-thumping hugs. "So, Jonnie," he said to her last of all, "any final questions?"

"Tell my last fortune." In a way, she would even miss that.

"Easy. Nothing to it. You'll have hard times ahead, but you'll have a wonderful and exciting life."

"And where do you see all this? In your crystal ball?"

He tapped his forehead. "With my third eye. Can you see my third eye?"

"I can't see anything."

"You will," he said, "when you see the left eye of the donkey."

The door of the classroom closed behind them. They went home.

11

All the Little Birds
Come Home to Roost

"Who left a box on our porch?"

"It's for me." If they thought they were doing her a favor by leaving her the box of cups, they were wrong. Because with the cups, the soft nostalgia of the past hours faded and the old treacheries rushed back. And with them the fear of anticipation. Not so much of Billy, even, but of her father. What would she say to her father? . . . All those lost years.

"At least her mother sent her something," said Ada glumly. "All my mother said was good riddance."

"She didn't!" said Maryanne. "I don't believe it!"

"She didn't," Ada admitted. "She just didn't say anything."

They understood what she meant. Not saying anything was worse.

"My mother cried and prayed all night," said Maryanne. "My father told me never to darken his door. What does that mean, *darken* his door?"

Nobody knew what it meant.

"He said I was ungrateful, that he gave me everything, and

143

I didn't appreciate. I'm praying to the Virgin to make me more grateful."

Ada was getting depressed about her mother. It was easy to get depressed about mothers, and they had to cheer her up because she was going to court to pick up her boyfriend *if*, and they couldn't take a chance on jinxing it with bad feelings. "It's this way," said Jonnie. "The house is a new life. A new world, wide on either side. It's a different kind of luck here."

Ada looked up at the house, where the eyes blinked at her through bright windows. "I wish my grandma was here."

"Maybe she is," said Maryanne. "You said the Indian god believes in spirits. So if your grandma was the only one who gave a damn about you, she's probably a spirit now, and she's probably here watching you."

Ada's broad face broke into a grin. It was only when Ada smiled and it changed her face that you realized how seldom she did. "I wouldn't put it past that old lady. So I'll be right back after the hearing. Keep the coffee pot boiling. I'll be here, with or without." They all knocked the wood of their front door. "It better be *with*."

It was her old bed made up with fresh sheets. It was her old pillow, but placed so that it would face the sea. She cranked the windows open to the sky. The ocean air washed the room clean, scoured it with the tang of salt and seaweed. The crisp air brought its own energy, and lightened her with it. The room itself was sunlight. Outside, birds wheeled and squawked. She marveled at how they caught the air and soared on wind. She had never seen a happier sight in her life, those birds floating on air, nothing stopping them, hanging against gravity, and then, when they wanted to, dropping, caught by the arm of the air itself and flung out again, seaward. She thought of the Friday goddesses, Frigga and Freyja, who watched over women. They came as birds. They knew the future, but they wouldn't tell.

She thought about how odd it was that things you learned colored and changed other things you thought you knew. She laid her green glass egg on the window seat where it could catch the light. She put her father's painted clock beside it. The birds dipped and floated, watching her, but telling nothing. It came to her that she would put her baby's cradle near the window, to be watched over by the birds, and that she would paint the cradle with Thalia's butterflies.

In a way those were messages, those ideas. So maybe there was some prophecy in the leather-bound book. Somewhere there had to be the answer. Someplace. She touched the cover with her fingers . . .

A message came. But it came as a little fantasy. Lark was a real bird, soaring on the wind above their house, catching the breeze and soaring. If Lark were a bird truly, she would need a world wide and high, not flat where you couldn't breathe all the time. She would have a sky as high as the soul was high. It was true! She didn't understand it, but she knew exactly what it meant.

Maryanne's excited voice broke her reverie. "Arthur! He's here! In my own house!"

Arthur Hammerman slouched through the kitchen, big-eyed with wonder. "I can't believe a kitchen without *her* in it making me nervous."

Maryanne followed him at heel, like a puppy, hovering over him, stirring powdered coffee into his cup, settling her loving eyes on his acned face. "I don't even know how he takes his *cof*fee," she marveled. "Here he is the father of my baby and I don't even know if he takes sugar or cream or what."

"Four spoons," he said, "and lots of cream."

Nobody had remembered to buy cream.

He sipped his coffee like a king. He pulled Maryanne down on his lap and kissed her in gratitude.

"I told you," said a joyful almost tearful Maryanne. "I told you he had good qualities." She hugged and kissed his face. "So what does your mother say about me. Does she *like* me, do you think?"

"She doesn't even like *me*," said Arthur.

Billy Veller's boots clattered on the porch. His presence filled the doorway. "Jonnie!" He waited, arms outstretched, for her to come to him.

Billy had come home. She knew that she had been praying for this, to see him standing at her own door holding arms out to her. From the first day she met him, that had been her fantasy. But unbidden by her, court came into session. Her mother's voice argued in strident accusing tones. *Bum . . . he's a bum . . . I know Billy Veller.* Her baby humped and turned, but only a subjective witness now, hugging its *own* pouch, claiming its *own* space. It was her father who came forward to speak for Billy. *I never deserted you, did I, Jonnie? A father would never give up his own child . . .*

Billy stood there holding his arms out to her. She had seen it a thousand times in pictures, where the girl runs to the boy in slow motion, her hair flying behind her in the wind. But the heavy weight of her baby had made her slow and awkward. All she could do was walk to him and let him hold her. Billy Veller was home.

146

He released her finally because he had to deal with the house. It was new to him. He moved around the room, trying to understand its dimensions. He stretched out his arms, feeling for space. He squinted as he looked at it, as if the bright sunlight were his natural element, and the inside cramped him so that he had to tense up to take it in.

She brought him into the kitchen to meet Arthur Hammerman, since they were all family. She waited to see his reaction to Arthur. Billy shook hands with Arthur, and then put an arm around his shoulder and said a few friendly things. The whole court observed. You couldn't be a bum and be that kind to Arthur Hammerman. The court conferred, was sympathetic, but deferred verdict until it had one final irrevocable piece of evidence.

"Would you like to come up now and see my room?"

He nodded and followed. She felt the heavy imprint of his heels on the steps behind her. He followed her into the room and closed the door.

They faced each other finally — she and Billy Veller, who was the father of her baby. In the intimacy of the room, there was a sudden shyness between them. They walked to the window and looked out toward the sea. You could see that he was tired. He left her standing there watching the water and stretched out on her bed, boots and all. When she turned to him, his head was on her pillow, his arm flung out against the sheets of her bed. His smile was that same sad crooked smile. He held a hand out to her. "Come here."

She watched him from where she stood, her hands resting on the house that held her baby. "Did you like the name I picked for the baby?"

"Come here," he said again.

The baby turned and made its clear statement. "I called her Lark. So is that okay with you?"

147

The hand that reached for her relaxed and went limp against the pillow. "Was it a good idea to name it, honey, since we're giving it away?"

She turned cold, to the heart. Her baby stirred, protested. *When*, the Fates murmured, *when did we promise you that? You asked for Billy.*

The little Chevy coughed and chugged into the driveway, sputtered and stopped. "Ada's back!"

"See Ada later." He was still waiting for her. "There's something we have to get straight, Jonnie."

"Ada's back! I have to see if they let her boyfriend off." She slipped out of the room. *Not yet. She wasn't ready.* She had to prepare. It must be said right so that he would clearly understand. She heard him coming after her. But she wasn't *ready!* Everything had worked out, everything that had been promised. For once in her life she had wanted something and asked for something. For once, she had been petitioner to the Fates. And they had granted, beneficently, to the letter. But there was one thing she hadn't asked for, hadn't dared ask for. She heard Billy's heels coming after her. But she had to see if Ada was all right, didn't she?

"This here is Greyhorse." Ada made a formal introduction, presenting him to everyone.

Greyhorse must have been six feet three at least. Huge, broad, red-faced, high-cheeked, handsome — but like Ada, unsmiling. It was Billy who was most comfortable with him. Billy shook his hand solemnly and asked about his tribe. Billy had known many Indians. *So that was a sign, wasn't it?* Then why did her baby move and turn uneasily?

"Oglala Sioux." Greyhorse looked uneasily toward Ada. "If there's any of them left."

Maryanne had to shove Arthur forward to shake hands.

"Anybody got a beer?" asked Greyhorse.

"He doesn't need a beer," said Ada. "I'll make him some coffee."

Billy and Greyhorse moved to a corner of the room, talking about something. Arthur looked nervously on. Billy reached out, took Arthur by the shoulder and included him. Jonnie pointed that out to the court. That Billy understood what it meant to be left out, his kindness in including.

Ada walked in from the kitchen, stirring a cup of coffee. But her hands seemed nervous and unsteady. Something was wrong. She didn't seem to want to meet Jonnie's eyes.

Greyhorse was explaining something to Billy and Arthur. Billy offered Greyhorse a cigarette and lit it for him.

"What's wrong with everybody?" Jonnie asked. "Is this a celebration or not? Greyhorse is out!"

There was no air of celebration.

"Is he out or isn't he?"

"Sort of," said Ada.

"How can anybody be *sort of* out?" asked Maryanne.

"He's out *if*," said Ada.

"If *what*?"

Greyhorse had turned away and stood looking out of the window, his cigarette unsmoked and burning down.

Jonnie knew before the explanation! The Fates rumbled in that room. *We warned . . . you asked for too much . . . you asked for more than we bargained . . .*

"He's out if he goes into the army for two years," said Ada. "The judge says if he makes a good record for himself, it wipes him clean. He can even get into civil service."

"And if he *doesn't*?"

"He goes back to jail."

149

"What did you expect," said Billy. "They give it to you with one hand, and with the other they pull the rug out from under. What's a guy like him going to do in the army?"

"Let me get a gun in my hand," said Greyhorse. "I'll show you."

"He doesn't mean it," said Ada. "He's tired. He's got to figure out what to do."

"*Where* in the army? Here in L.A.? They have an army base down in Santa Ana or somewhere."

"Not here," said Ada.

"*Where* then? In Dakota? In the land of your people?"

"Have they got any Oglala Sioux in Fort Benning, Georgia?" asked Greyhorse.

Ada turned away.

"But if he has to go to Fort Benning, it means you'll have to have your baby without him!"

Greyhorse lowered himself into a chair near the window, sat watching the leaves of the eucalyptus making their patterns on the wall. He held the cigarette until the ash was almost ready to fall. He glanced at Ada with such sadness . . . and then looked away. "I'm going to Canada. I'll never make two years in the army."

"If he goes to Canada, he'll never come back." Ada looked desperately to Jonnie.

Jonnie *knew* what they were saying. She *knew* the look on Ada's face. She knew it all. *"But the house!"*

"We can't *make* it the two of us!" Maryanne's face was flushing and she was ready to cry. "My father told me never to darken his *door!* I *can't* go home now."

"I'm not going back on the house," said Ada, but her eyes were on Greyhorse. "I made a promise. I'll die before I'll break it." She held her baby with both hands. "I'll just

150

have to have it without him. Maybe he'll write me where he is."

"What's so important about a rented house?" asked Billy. "This guy's in trouble! He's had bad breaks! You know what it means to a guy to have bad breaks?"

"You don't know what's a rotten break," said Arthur, "until you meet my mother."

Jonnie couldn't stand it! She was going crazy! "What's *happening* to us? This is our *house! Our* place! We're *in* it!"

Ada rocked herself as if in mourning. "It's just that if he runs to Canada, I'm afraid he'll never come back."

". . . but the *house!*"

". . . he's got this restless thread in him . . ."

The room was static and airless. Maryanne moved to stand beside Jonnie, holding her hand. But Billy and Arthur stood by Greyhorse, waiting to see what Jonnie would say, hanging together like brothers, all of them like brothers.

"I'll die before I go back on my word," said Ada.

Jonnie looked at Ada and at Maryanne. The three of them looked at each other, a family of sisters. It was all said. It was clear as ice. They hugged each other and held each other.

"Look . . ." said Billy, "there are other houses. Why is this house so important?"

There *were* no other houses! Not for her!

But her love for Ada was stronger than the house. "You have to go with him." The words were stones, heavy in her chest. "You can't let him go alone."

Ada turned her face away. "You'll have to send me. I'll never go by myself."

They stood and whispered together, the three of them, trying to understand. The old fears and insecurities moved in, and the what-ifs.

"What if it doesn't work out?" asked Jonnie. "What if you can't pull out that thread?"

Ada looked at her deeply, from a wide and unsmiling face. "What else have I *got*, Jonnie?"

"Okay if we take the car?" asked Greyhorse. "We'll sell it in Georgia and send the money back."

It was like tearing a living thing apart, into three pieces.

"I don't know what else to do," said Ada as they made their final parting. "I can't figure it any other way. And he's my baby's father. That's something, isn't it?"

"It's something," they consoled her.

"Somewhere there has to be a land of my people. Somewhere there has to be Indians to welcome us. Someplace there has to be a house for me."

They all knocked wood and wished it.

"I'll remember this house," said Ada. "I'll remember it all my life."

The little car chugged away — far away.

"*Now* what?" asked Maryanne, clutching her crucifix. "I think the Virgin must be sore because of the Christian Science. Who listens to Christian Scientists? I mean, if you're not Catholic, who *listens?*"

"I don't get all this fuss about an old house," said Billy. "There are a million houses, all over the world."

"This is *my* house," said Jonnie.

Then she remembered her father. "I think that's why my father is coming. Because it was known that I'd need help with the house. There's a reason, isn't there?" She looked to Maryanne for confirmation.

Maryanne shrugged. "Don't ask me. I don't have much faith in fathers.

"Look, kid," said Billy as they drove along. "Believe me. Don't count on people, especially if you haven't seen them for a long time."

"My father won't let me down." She looked at his face. "Would you let your daughter down?"

Billy parked the car in front of her house, turned on the radio, lit a cigarette and settled in for a wait.

"Come in with me."

"Not me," he said. "And if you were smart, honey, you wouldn't go in either."

She started to get out when she saw that Abel's car was still parked in the driveway. "What is *he* doing here! Come in with me, please! I'm scared, Billy."

"Not me," he said. "What I don't need is another father."

She realized in sudden panic that the last time her father had seen her was as a child. Would he recognize her? How was she to react to him? Run to him as a child, as she wanted to do? Sit on his lap and hug him and let him hug her, as she yearned for him to do? Or come to him as a pregnant woman, ready to have a child of her own?

The apartment itself seemed strange now, alien and remote, something from a former life. Abel and her mother sat drinking coffee at the kitchen table. They turned to her as she entered. Old angers stirred. Old arguments. She was tired of it. She just wanted her father now. And for the new life to begin. Now she wondered why her father wasn't with them. But he wouldn't be. He would be waiting for her alone. They would meet alone, after all these years, just the two of them.

She left Abel and her mother and hurried into the living room. But he wasn't there! Where? Where *was* he? She

153

ran down the hallway to her bedroom! But he wasn't anywhere!

He *had* to be! It had been *promised!*

When, murmured the Fates, *when* laughed the Fates. *You asked for Billy.*

Another one of her mother's tricks! She should have known better! She rushed back to the kitchen. She had let down her guard! She had trusted her mother's word! Fool! "What did you do! Send him away again! What did you say to him!"

Her mother was speechless against the assault.

"Leave your mother alone!" said Abel. "He didn't come."

"Liar!"

"He didn't come, Jonnie. He's never come. But she's been here. She's always been here."

"Liar!" she screamed. "He came and she sent him away again!"

"He's never been anything but a pack of letters," said Abel. "Only letters. She hated to have to make you understand that. But you'll have to understand it now, and accept it. And stop blaming her."

She saw the letter on the table. Special delivery. She knew her father's hand.

"It came this morning," said Abel. "That's why we waited. To be here with you when you found it."

Her fingers were too thick to open it. She pulled the envelope apart to get at the letter. The same, the old familiar slant of the lines, the shape of the words.

Dear Jonnie:

She prayed. She put into motion every magical formula of her life, every incantation. That *this* time would be different!

The house rose in her fantasy . . . waiting . . . a shimmering dream which in a few words on a page would either become her reality, her new life . . . or dissipate . . . like everything else.

> Dear Jonnie: When she wrote me at first, telling me what had happened . . .

She had to stop to read the line again . . . and again. She didn't understand it. She looked to her mother, who was hanging on to Abel, watching her, watching her face. "Did he *know* about me? *Before* this?"

"Please . . ." begged her mother, ". . . he couldn't understand . . . he wasn't here to see how it all happened."

> . . . I wanted to come back and kill the boy, or kill her for letting you run the streets . . .

"He'd been away too long," said her mother, as if she were apologizing for the words on the page. "He was too far away to understand how it was."

> . . . how could you have let me down, Jonnie? Did you ever stop to think how this would hurt me?

Their eyes were on her. She could sense the look on their faces. *Don't you feel sorry for me! You don't need to feel sorry for me!*

"He loved you, Jonnie. In his own way. In the only way he knew."

> She said you were moving out. I forbid it. I don't want you living anywhere where you can't be supervised. I'll be in touch with you as soon as I can. For now, I'm sending some money to buy something for yourself . . .

*

The bills were wrapped in paper. Ten dollar bills. Two of them. First she tore them in half, then in pieces, in shreds.

"She couldn't tell you," said Abel. "You wouldn't have believed her. He was all promises."

She didn't want to hear their voices anymore. She walked past them toward the door. She heard them coming after her. *Don't you feel sorry for me!* She hurried. Billy was holding the car door open for her.

She slammed the door and they drove off.

Billy was almost angry with her. "What did I tell you! Why did you have to let yourself in for a thing like that? Grow up, honey."

"Just take me home," she said.

"Poor kid." He put an arm around her as he drove. "You think I don't know what it's like . . ."

The wind blew against her face. She didn't feel it. The noise of traffic blurred. She hardly heard what he was saying. She knew he wanted to comfort her. At least she had that now. She saw the kindness in Billy Veller. At least he was here. She had that much. But she had been fighting the Fates. She had been fighting her luck. They were liars who told her that luck did not exist, that knocking wood was a fool's game. She had been defiant, but she knew better now. Billy was talking to her, trying to soothe her. Billy was all she had left now.

But it wasn't enough!

She wanted her baby! She wanted her house!

They were alike, he said as they drove. As peas in a pod.

She only wanted to be back at the house, in her room, to try to understand it.

". . . you and me, Jonnie. You can count on me, you know that, and I can count on you. So we'll take our little stake . . ."

". . . what stake?" she asked numbly.

156

". . . from the baby. We'll get a good lawyer. There are people who'd pay plenty to adopt a baby. We could get maybe three or four thousand."

She didn't hear what he was saying.

He turned a corner and parked in front of the house.

"Maybe more, if we're lucky. This town is used up, for both of us. We'll go to Europe maybe. Maybe to Greece."

"You want to sell my baby," she said.

He pulled his arm away. "Don't be crazy! I didn't say *sell!*"

The house was dark. Maryanne and Arthur were gone. She fumbled in her purse for the key.

"It's just that a lawyer fixes these things up, and we're giving it up anyhow, so why not get our expenses out of it at least. And then we'll see where the wind takes us."

"You want to sell my *baby!*" She got out of the car and started toward the house.

"Are you *crazy*, saying a thing like that!"

She heard him start after her. She climbed the porch steps and opened the door. She heard her mother's voice calling her, a car swerve to the curb. *"You want to sell my baby!"* she screamed. She walked inside and locked the door behind her.

He pounded the door. "What do you think you're *doing!*

"Jonnie!" her mother called.

But she was safe inside now. It was all behind her.

The house welcomed her. Empty, soft, dark . . . it welcomed her. Outside, the door rattled. They called her name. She didn't even hear them anymore because she was safe at last. The house was hers now. Just hers. She stood alone in the darkness, the soft darkness. The room whispered to her, in a rustle of bird's wings. Outside, they screamed for her. But they were all behind her. She was at one with her house. Everything else was cushioned, softened by the widening space between her and the world. She walked through the dark room with its rustling voices . . . old familiar voices, with their soft, rustling hush of consolation. Joan Fontaine, in *Jane Eyre*, softly telling the sad tale of her blind lover. Bette Davis, learning that she was dying of blindness. She climbed the stairs with the old queens of England, who climbed to the gallows with heads held high. Friday was hanging day. Her old queens helped her to climb. The warmth of the house was still there, but the fires were dying. She walked like a queen, holding the rail to support herself. She knew now the meaning of her destiny. All of it. The house, her father, her foolish dream of love that did not exist. *Fool,* they said in soft derisive laughter. She entered the room and closed the door. *Big fool.* The windows were open. Downstairs, in another world, she heard the shattering of glass. No, *they* were the fools. They didn't understand that it was too late now. Through her open window wind washed in from the sea. The moon, its big sad face, like Antoinette's round face, brightened the room. *Fool* not to have known that nothing existed . . . that the world as she envisioned it did *not* exist. But this *room* existed. She walked around the room to touch the solidity of the walls for the last time, around and around until she was dizzy. Then even the walls ceased to be solid, because she didn't understand anymore what was fantasy and what was real. She leaned out of the window, drawn to the sea. The piercing edge of sea air made her shiver. She heard them crashing around the house, calling for her. They would all be sorry . . . all the liars. She leaned out of the window, giddy now. She had only to yield herself to gravity, to let go, to fall, to roll down the slope until she reached the embracing arms of the sea, where the waves would lap her up, carry her out, where she would sink like a stone, into the warm waters, to be soothed as she descended by tendrils of seaweed, to float with the curious fishes, to become part of the softness and the comfort of the waters. She opened the window wider, and leaned out, almost fell. She tried to gather this last ounce of courage from all the queens of the late-lates who had lifted their hair for the ax of the executioner. The winds of her final destiny brushed her face, whispered to her, urged her to show her bravery, her dignity at last . . .

Her life passed before her. She saw the rescue boat dragging the water for her body. Her father at the helm with the captain, frantically scanning the choppy seas. *All my fault,* her father moaned. The sailors pulled in their nets. *It's her . . . God, look at what the sharks have done to her!* She couldn't bear it! Quickly she erased it. Doors were slamming below. She leaned over the window ledge, trying to find the courage. The boat cut through the now calm waters. The sun shone, gulls swooped. Her father nervously paced the deck. Her mother, in black, sat crying. Billy squatted on a pile of rope, his head in his hands. *If only she had waited, if she had let me explain . . . she didn't understand . . .* They all ran to the rail while the sailors brought up her frozen lifeless body. Tenderly they lifted her aboard. Her father pushed through the crowd of stunned onlookers. *Let me take her . . .* Billy shoved her father aside, lifted her lifeless body, looked down at the stilled face. *I couldn't have her in life . . . she's mine in death . . .*

Hurry, whispered the voices . . .

The mourners filled the pews of the chapel, silently weeping. Her father sat alone, consumed with remorse. She lay in the oak coffin, marble white, the faintest blush painted on the hollows of her cheeks, her hands crossed on her breast. Slowly the mourners filed past, looked down, sobbing. Her father's face bent over her. *Jonnie, I'll never forgive myself. You didn't understand how much I loved you, but I was weak* . . . Billy had collapsed at the side of the coffin. The minister stepped forward. *Nobody understood Joanna Olson, how much she suffered in her brief life, what she thought, what she felt, how much she wanted to live and be happy* . . .

It went off. The whole picture clicked off.

She stepped back from the window, frightened by the height, her heart pounding. She wanted to *live*, not to *die! She wanted to live in this house, not die in it!* She must have been *crazy* . . . what she almost did to herself and her baby.

"Jonnie! Where are you!"

She was dizzy to fainting. Suddenly the sensation of warmth and wet spread down her legs. What was happening . . . she reached down — her hand was wet. *Something was breaking! Something was wrong! Something was wrong with her baby!* "Mother . . ." she called. The ache started in her back. She begged her baby to wait, it wasn't time. But the wet spread down her legs and the heaviness pressed her and the egg that held her baby cracked and came apart. It was too soon! *"Mommy . . ."* she screamed, *". . . help me . . ."*

160

12

Hope Is a Small Bird Singing . . .

NOW SHE WAS in the hands of strangers.

They rolled her along the white sterile corridors, lifted her, moved her, robot hands taking possession of her entirely. She was alone — and in pain. When it hurt, she screamed.

"Relax." A nurse patted her perfunctorily on the shoulder. "Or the medication won't be effective."

"Where's my doctor!" she screamed.

"Your doctor will come. You're not ready for him yet. Just relax."

"It hurts me!" she screamed. "*You* climb up here and have pains and *you* relax! I need to go to the bathroom!"

The nurse pushed her firmly back. "No you don't. It's just pressure. Relax and let your baby do its work." The nurse turned away, busied herself with something else. Nobody cared that she was in pain . . . nobody came with solace and comfort . . . everything was gone . . . nothing remained . . . and she *screamed!*

The nurse bent over her sternly. "How old are you?"

"Sixteen!" she wept. "I'm only sixteen . . ."

"If you're old enough to be having a baby, it's time for you to grow up."

She curled into her ball of pain and held her baby.

Her baby, her *baby*, so long protected in its little bed of water, like a fish safe in her private pool, was not protected anymore. Now she saw her baby fighting to leave her, as everybody and everything else had left her. The long and tortuous route through her body, through caves and tunnels that weren't even full-grown and too small. She wanted to blow up the whole world. She wanted to obliterate the whole world in one big explosion and leave only the darkness and silence of nothing. But the baby pressed against her bones, needing to be out.

She gave up.

She lay back and let the pain roll through her as if she were a hollow shell. Her brain detached itself, and so the pain didn't concern her any longer. The pain rolled on doing something of its own. Out of this cotton-wool world, Robert Frost came to her. Dumb Robert Frost. *Miles to go before I sleep, and promises to keep . . . Miles to go before I sleep and promises to keep . . .* She reached through the fog for a last communication with her baby, while they were still one. "Don't worry," she said to her baby, "I've kept my promises to you at least."

The doctor was bending over her, holding her hand. "Sorry I had to take so long."

The world returned in a blur of anger. "What did you do, stop for coffee while I was *dying* here?"

He pressed her hand. "Relax. Try to relax. Don't fight it."

Somebody bent over her to put a mask against her face. She was frightened. "Please . . ." she begged. "Don't hurt me!"

162

"It's only oxygen, to wake your baby up."

She breathed in cold fierce drafts of air. She was climbing a birch tree to subdue the branches, and she launched out too soon, and it *hurt* her. She breathed, and it came to her with crystal clarity. She walked through a pathless wood and a twig cut her eye, when it was open, and it *hurt* her.

Her body felt numb, but she was conscious of a terrible sense of loss. *They were taking her baby.*

With a rush, like the flight of birds, her baby left her.

He held up the bloody thing. "A girl."

"It's dead . . ." she said.

She heard the small cry.

"A little early, but she's fine . . . a beauty."

She didn't believe it. She lifted her head to see. She had a baby. She lay back and closed her eyes. She didn't want to see them cut the cord.

The doctor bent over her. "She's small, but she's healthy. Why are you crying?"

"I'm all alone . . ." she wept.

"How could you be all alone? Your mother and father are pacing out there. Some young man is smoking himself sick."

The nurse held the baby for her to see. She turned her head away.

"*Why*, Jonnie, when you've waited all these months?"

"You wouldn't understand," she wept.

She fought against awakening. She wanted to stay forever in the warmth of the dream. She came to consciousness slowly, half-dazed, stiff, her body ached and her stitches pulled. The whiteness of the room hurt her eyes. It was moments before she realized that someone, a man, was sitting beside her.

She groped for her old fantasy! None of what had happened was real! Her father had come! The letter had been the lie!

Her eyes cleared.

She had been tricked again. *Abel.*

The last joke on her. Everything gone. Everything finished. And now she was going to get a lecture from Abel. The last pitiful joke.

"How are you feeling, Jonnie?"

She tried to pull herself up, but she was still dizzy.

"I wanted to see you before I left. Is there anything I can do for you?"

The enormity of the insult overwhelmed her. It wasn't fair! She had been cheated out of everything. *Just a big joke on me.* She heard the Fates laughing. But she would die before she let anybody see her cry. "There's nothing you can do. Just leave me alone now." She meant it. She wanted to be free of all of them. "I don't need anything, or anyone. Not anymore."

He kept his pale eyes on her face. "Then you must be made out of iron. Not like the rest of us."

"I don't need her and I don't need you. So tell her I'm okay now, and she can go. I was scared for a while, but I'm okay now. Thank her and tell her so long."

"She wants to stay around with you for a couple of weeks, until you're stronger."

"I don't want her to." She wished that he would leave. She wanted them all to leave. She had herself. And that was all she wanted now. "Tell her she can go. I don't need a martyr hanging over me. Let her work her fingers to the bone over you."

"It's not just her," said Abel. "It's him you're mad at. It

164

was rotten that your father didn't come. But she tried to tell you what kind of man he was. Don't hurt yourself because of him, Jonnie. Not anymore. Just let him go."

But she couldn't let her father go. Not even now. She groped for the security of her father's remembered face. And she didn't want Abel talking him down. "You leave my father *out* of this!"

"Accept it the way it is, Jonnie. Let him go. He can only hurt you."

She put her hands up over her ears.

"I can't make your father into something he's not. But she's here, Jonnie. And I'm here. Is it a terrible weakness to admit you need somebody?"

She pressed her hands over her ears. "I don't need anybody! I don't want anybody anymore! Don't you understand me!"

"Is it so hard to take somebody's hand when they want to give it to you?"

"Liars!" she said.

"Would you know the truth from a lie? Would you recognize the truth if you heard it?"

She shut her ears. *Your destiny*, whispered the Fates, *your destiny is to have no hand except what we choose to give you . . . at our whim . . . when it pleases . . .*

"I got lucky when I met your mother, Jonnie. I want to make a family with her. And you're part of that family. If you had to come to us . . ."

"Don't you understand that I don't *want* you?"

". . . if you had to come to us, you wouldn't have to fight for it or scream for it . . ."

She tried to block him out!

". . . or scream for it or use that sharp tongue, just because

165

you need what everybody needs. Why are you so hard on yourself?"

She had her ears closed, but she heard him just the same. She wanted to reach out and hit him, pound at him, and smash him with her fists.

But even as she did, she knew that he had told her the truth.

She tried in the terrible white light of that room to see the nothing of his pale nothing face, but she only saw a kindly man with soft eyes.

They make you promises, the Fates laughed, *and they let you down.*

"We're not so different, Jonnie. You need a family. I need a family. Come with us if you want to. If you need to come, then come. No questions. And you'd be welcome."

"Really!" she said. "Really! You'd just love having me come along on your honeymoon, wouldn't you."

"I said you'd be welcome. I meant it. But come as a friend. Give me a chance with you, Jonnie. It's not easy standing between two battling women."

Trust it, they laughed. *Big fool . . .*

He sat smiling at her, a kindly soft-eyed man. "I've got news for you. The war is over."

In the end, she didn't even need to cover her ears because the voices faded. She had known it all along. She knew it at that moment when she stood by the window, when the voices tried to trick her. She knew that *they* were the liar. She knew then that luck was a fool's game.

Taking Abel's hand was the hardest thing she ever did in her life. Her arm was like iron, as if *they* still held on to it. But in the end, she bent and wept against him because she knew he was telling the truth and for once in her life, for *once* she had a right to have somebody holding her and comforting her and taking away the monsters that rumbled in closets while she slept. She was exhausted now. She let him bring her some juice, and fix her bed, and sit beside her while she tried to understand what to do. She needed to know the truth about other things. About a thousand things. "Is he a bum?" she asked. "Is he a liar?"

"The boy? That's a hurt boy. Not a liar. And I'll tell you the truth, I've been knocked around too much in my life to call down any man. I'd hate to see him hurt. So ask yourself a hard question. Can you give that boy what he needs? Can he give you what you need? You've got a whole life and a child, and a child's whole life. Those are questions she can't answer for you and I can't answer for you. You'll have to find the answers for yourself."

She knew that.

"But, whichever way it goes, you have somebody waiting to give you a hand if you take a spill."

In the terrible white light of that room, she knew that also.

Billy Veller came into the room carrying roses.

She couldn't look at him yet. She saw him sit down beside her holding the bunch of roses, the thorny ends wrapped in foil, clutching the foil end in his hands. When she turned to him finally, she saw the old familiar hurt eyes.

She tried to reach over to touch his face. He drew away. "You should never have said that to me." The eyes accused her. "I would never have made you do anything you didn't want. I thought we trusted each other. I thought we knew better than to go back on each other. What else do we *have?*" He was looking at the roses as he spoke to her. "I almost died knowing that you were hurting in there, and I couldn't help

167

you. If you had just said you didn't want to take money for it, then okay. We could have talked about it. If you want to give it up for nothing, I won't fight you on it. It would have been a little stake, though, to get us started. So, okay. We'll figure out another way." She saw him looking into the roses, trying to make a new pattern of it. "I'll see what I can scrape up here in L.A. Then, after you give it up, we'll see where the wind takes us. I have plans, Jonnie. I have big ideas you don't even know yet. It would have been easier with the money from the baby, but, if that's the way you want it, you call it, honey." The green eyes of Billy Veller told his whole story. *I don't want to be alone again.*

She lay back and looked at the both of them in the mirror . . . through the looking glass. Two people she had never seen before. He was a tall thin boy with sad eyes. Nothing Viking, nothing noble about his face. Just a plain hurt boy.

She saw Ada embracing her wounded Indian.

She saw Maryanne hanging on to Arthur, who was forever tied to his mother, hanging on because there was nothing else. But that way you hung on to *something* at least, even though it hurt you, because if you let go, what *was* there? She looked at her own face in the mirror. She was a pale, unfinished girl. She hadn't realized she was so young. She remembered the fantasy. She wanted to jump on Billy and hug him and make him laugh again. But she looked hard at his face. His face was like a still portrait of somebody she had once known. The story of his face was already written . . . his whole life was written. She understood in the cold white light of the room what it meant to be a *real* woman, loving a *real* man, not a fantasy summer boy but a lonely man who sat gripping the thorn ends of roses and dreaming his own dreams.

"One of these days I'll hit it, Jonnie. It's just a matter of one good break."

She knew what the two roads were now that diverged in the yellow wood. One where you held the tiger by the tail, because the tiger was the only friend you had, but the tail whipped you around and you suffered all the blows according to what luck decreed.

The other path was thorny. But you walked it by putting one of your own feet in front of the other.

She reached up to touch his face. "I'll always love you, but I can't give up my baby."

He came to a slow realization of what she was saying. Maybe he had always known it, but he was hearing it for the first time now. The hurt welled in his eyes, accusing her . . . *she had promised . . . from that first phone call she had promised . . .*

"I lied," she said. "I can't give the baby up. The baby is a piece of me. It's not something I *can* give up."

"But I haven't got a buck in my pocket! I *can't* take care of a baby! And I need you, Jonnie! I need *you!* I! *I* need . . ."

In the clear white light of the room, she understood what only a real woman could understand . . . that she had *hurt* him.

"There are places I want to show you . . ." He was pleading now, begging. "I've been to those places alone . . . and I need *some*body . . ."

"I can't give up the baby."

Tears filled his eyes. "Don't let me down . . . not you . . ."

"I wouldn't want to let you down . . . I'd try not to let you down . . . but sooner or later I would . . . and in sixteen years, she would. And I can't take that chance."

She prayed that he would understand. He threw the roses on the bed. He started to say something, but couldn't. Just gave her a long look she would remember all her life, and walked away.

There was still time to go after him! To catch him and hold him and have him hold her. To soothe him and comfort him. But he was gone now, not physically, but *forever* gone. All she had left of him was a bunch of roses, little buds of roses that would soon be brown. So she understood everything now.

But what good was it to understand? The emptiness pressed in worse than death. The flowers were there and he was not. The flowers did not console her. What good were flowers when the world was *empty!* What good was anything? *April comes like an idiot, babbling and strewing flowers.* In her mind's eye, the teacher came and sat at the side of the bed.

Are you satisfied! wept Jonnie, accusing.

I didn't want you to learn this way.

I'm nothing! I'm alone! Is that what you wanted, for me to know I'm nothing!

You ate the apple, said the teacher, *now you can grow up.*

I'm empty . . .

Now you can begin to fill the cup up to the brim, and *above the brim.*

Her mother walked in and dispelled the vision. "I saw him leave. Thank God you used a little sense."

She didn't want to discuss it, or explain it. She was too tired to be angry with anyone. She didn't want to wrangle with her mother, not anymore, but she still ached from all the years of her life.

"I know it's hard, Jonnie, but it's best to give him up."

"I gave *him* up! But I'm *not* giving up my baby!"

"You drive me crazy!" said her mother. "Did you think I could ask you to give away your baby any more than I could

170

give *you* away? Although Lord knows it would be easier all the way around."

"Why didn't you!" The old sarcasm seeped back into her voice. "Why *didn't* you! You dumped my father easy enough. Why didn't you dump me too! It would have been easier, all the way around."

Her mother looked puzzled. "Because I love you."

"Love," she mimicked. "And when did you stop? When I turned out to be such a failure!"

Her mother searched for a Kleenex, couldn't find one, gave up finally, and sat defeated at the side of Jonnie's bed. She tried to look at Jonnie but couldn't. She looked at the wilting roses. "You're stronger than I am, Jonnie. I should have sent your father away. I didn't . . . not soon enough. I was lonely, just like you. So I stuck with him. He hurt me, every day of my life. Not because he was bad, or cruel, or unkind. It was just because he never made me feel less alone. But then I had you, didn't I. My own sweet baby. You were so comforting. But then you got older, and you wanted something also. Something? You wanted *every*thing! And suddenly I wasn't getting anything for myself. Nothing was left for me. I was left *out*. And I was bitter. When I understood that, finally, when I understood what had happened, it was too late. He was gone, and you were closed against me, like stone. All I could do was to batter against that stone door, begging to be let in. All of you, with your babies, all you children with babies, you don't understand what babies are. They're *you*, Jonnie, sixteen years later. Wait sixteen years . . ."

Her mother sat rummaging through a pocket for a Kleenex she needed. A woman looking tired and lonely. What her mother said cut through walls, through steel, almost broke her heart.

"Come with me . . . with Abel and me."

She knew she couldn't do that. "I can't . . . I have my own place now. I have a place of my own."

"But you don't have it. Most of the girls are gone."

"I have a month, at least. I can see what works out."

"There's nothing *to* work out! You're a sixteen-year-old girl! You can't do it by yourself!"

"You did."

They looked at each other strangely. Her mother seemed the helpless one. How could she ever have been so angry at such a helpless lady.

"Who will take care of you if you're ill? What if the bills don't get paid! What if something happens to the baby!"

Fear descended with the what-ifs.

But then . . . what if she could find other sisters to share the house? What if Maryanne would hold steadfast until things worked out? What if even now Thalia were on a train somewhere, with her stolen baby, headed back to the butterflies that were rightly hers? What if they could transfer Greyhorse, who was going to make Fort Benning a *lot* of trouble, back to L.A., near Santa Ana or somewhere? What if that smart lawyer would swing it? "What if you came and stayed with me for a while, until I got the hang of it, until I figure things out."

Her mother nodded yes. What passed between them couldn't be spoken in words. It was stronger than words. She knew that her mother wanted to kiss her or something, but neither of them knew how.

The door shoved open. The doctor's nurse pushed her starched self into the room carrying magazines and an ice cream carton. "*So* . . ." she laughed in her annoying high fruity voice, "how are we all feeling this morning? Are our stitches feeling all right?"

172

Her mother was searching desperately for Kleenex, and the stitches hurt. All she needed now was the Daughter of Dracula! The old hard angry words bubbled to the surface and exploded. *"Our* stitches hurt like *hell!* What does he tie, sailor knots!"

The nurse looked dismayed, but smiled indulgently. "Doctor said you were the only woman he ever delivered who asked for chocolate almond fudge under anesthetic. You looked so young, he wasn't sure whether he'd delivered your baby or taken out your tonsils. So I thought since you had such a hard time of it . . ." She handed Jonnie the carton and a spoon.

The melted chocolate ran in swirls with the melted whipped cream. The prissy, thin-lipped nurse, in spite of the reproof, was actually watching to see if she was enjoying it. In the terrible clear light of that room, she understood that the ice cream was a gift of love and that the nurse was just someone, like the rest of them, trying to bumble her way through, trying to make a place for herself. "I'm sorry." She dipped the spoon into the ice cream. "Toads come from my mouth."

"So," smiled the nurse, "are we all *right* then?"

Jonnie licked the sweet spoon and looked at the strange familiar woman sitting beside her. "I think I'm all right . . . my mother is here."

"Oh Jonnie . . ." said her mother, with tenderness.

"Oh Jonnie . . ." she mimicked, but softly.

The game was over. "I want to see my baby now."

Her baby was under glass, not ready to emerge. A sweet baby, soft as a rosebud, white skin and fine dark hair. Under the skin, Jonnie could see little veins that carried Lark's blood, and Jonnie's blood, and her mother's blood, like a roadmap of the generations. Little hands with sculptured fingers, nails like the insides of oyster shells. New dreams of the outside world puzzled her . . . she frowned . . . and then smiled again for some private reasons . . . and slept again, dreaming of that safe and wonderful house she had lived in.

"Well," said Jonnie to her daughter, "there's another fine mess we got ourselves into."

She lay back against the cool sheets and wondered what it meant to be a mother. For one thing, she would have to stop biting her nails. She waited for that *different* feeling to come over her. It didn't. She tried to arm herself with common sense, like Benjamin Franklin. *Spend one cent less than your clear gains.* She realized that she didn't even know *how* to take care of a baby. She wondered if she breast-fed, would it embarrass her. She thought about the terrible twos. She would be eighteen then. How would she be able to meet new people, with a baby? How would she be able to learn the new things she had to learn? The baby had to be cared for and rent had to be paid and dinners cooked. It frightened her.

On the other hand, there was her sweet daughter lying in a crib painted with butterflies, reaching out a hand to touch her face, smiling up at her, waiting for her to smile in return, her own flesh and blood child. Or leaving the house to go shopping or somewhere, her baby would be slung across her back Indian style, close to her as she walked, and later to be talked to and sung to and taught, all the things they could learn together, and that daughter would be a permanent bond with her, no matter what happened, no matter what transient angers. Forever linked to her.

She saw the unfinished picture of herself in the mirror, and she wondered what she might become. She let herself drift.

174

She pictured herself on a ship sailing out to sea. She was taller now, and willowy, with long hair that lay across her shoulders. She saw from the corner of her eye the young man who stared at her with unabashed admiration, a handsome face with soft, generous eyes. He moved toward her, smiled a funny smile — like Robert Redford's, boyish and happy, or Jimmy Caan's. *Forgive me . . . I had to talk to you . . . Did you ever feel that you had met someone before? Do you believe in Fate?*

She would have to give it up in stages. She wanted to get back to her house, to her room, to show it to her baby. She knew there were hard times ahead, but there were good times too. And why not? She deserved them, didn't she? She was sixteen, and alive, and a mother, and a mother's daughter — and she had made choices. And that, after all, was something.